S0-BYG-204

SOCCER

The ultimate guide to the beautiful game

CLIVE GIFFORD

KINGFISHER

LONDON & NEW YORK

Foreword

Soccer is a wonderful game, a sport that knows
no boundaries of race, age, wealth, sex, or religion.
Soccer is a sport that reaches everyone. All over
the world, people young and old play it, watch
it, and read about it. This book captures the
international appeal, enjoyment, and excitement
of this unique sport.

People often forget that for all its drama
and beauty soccer is a simple game
built on a set of individual skills, allied to
working together as a team. Although natural
ability is a gift, players are not born with these
skills and understanding—they are things
that must be learned. To be a success requires
much hard work, patience, self-sacrifice, and
a desire to study the game and improve. Most
importantly, it involves loving what you do.
Young people will continue to play and watch
soccer, and this book will help to increase their
enjoyment of the world's most beautiful game.

Copyright © Macmillan Publishers International 2002, 2020
First published 2002 in the United States by Kingfisher
This edition published 2020 by Kingfisher,
120 Broadway, New York, NY 10271
Kingfisher is an imprint of Macmillan Children's Books, London.
All rights reserved.

Kingfisher books are available for special promotions and premiums.
For details contact: Special Markets Department, Macmillan,
120 Broadway, New York, NY 10271

For more information, please visit
www.kingfisherbooks.com

Printed in China
10 9 8 7 6 5 4 3 2 1
1TR/1019/WKT/UG/128MA

Distributed in the U.S. and Canada by Macmillan,
120 Broadway, New York, NY 10271

LIBRARY OF CONGRESS CATALOGING-IN-PUBLICATION DATA
Gifford, Clive.
  Soccer / by Clive Gifford. — 2nd ed.
    p. cm.
  Includes index
  Summary: Presents the game of soccer, including its basic rules, structure, playing positions, needed
skills, and great players.
    1. Soccer—Juvenile literature. [1. Soccer.] I. Title
GV943.25 .G55 2002
796.334—dc21   2001038939

ISBN 978-0-7534-7547-8

Author: Clive Gifford
Consultant: Anthony Hobbs

Contents

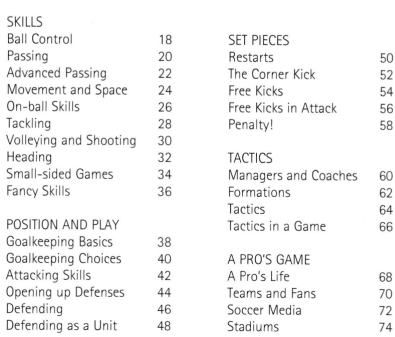

The Global Game

Goal, *gola*, *gol*! Whichever language you speak, a game of soccer provides 90 minutes or more of adrenaline-pumping action, intense drama, and breathtaking skills. Soccer is a game that can be played in a park, on a beach, or in a huge stadium watched on television by millions of people. But wherever it is played, soccer inspires powerful emotions and fierce loyalties like no other game on earth.

▶ Brazilian legend Ronaldo grew up in a poor district of Rio de Janeiro. He secured a place on Brazil's 1994 World Cup team at the age of 18. He went on to play for some of the world's most famous teams—Barcelona, Real Madrid, and AC Milan. In 2006 he became the highest scorer in World Cup history, with 15 goals at the finals, a record that was later beaten by now retired German striker Miroslav Klose, with 16.

▲ Soccer crosses all boundaries. It is passionately followed by men, women, boys, and girls of all ages and backgrounds. Television allows even the remotest places to have access to games from around the world.

Less is more

Soccer is essentially a simple game. The aim is to get the ball into the opponent's goal without using your hands or arms. Whichever team scores the most goals wins. Of course there are many rules and regulations, but these are designed to keep the game fair and flowing. Whatever your skill level, you can enjoy the game without expensive uniforms or equipment. You don't even need a soccer field. All you need for a friendly game is a safe, open space or indoor gym, along with a ball, a few players, and something to mark out a goal.

► Pelé described soccer as "the beautiful game." An outstanding Brazilian player from the late 1950s to the early 1970s, he is widely recognized as the greatest soccer player in the history of the game.

"Some people think football [soccer] is a matter of life and death. I don't like that attitude. I can assure them it is much more serious than that." Bill Shankly

"Football [soccer] is like a religion to me. I worship the ball, and I treat it like a god." Pelé

► Colorful supporters of the French national team cheer their side on at the final of the 2006 FIFA World Cup versus Italy. More than 600 million people tuned in to watch this game on TV.

Big business

Big teams, such as Spain's Real Madrid, England's Manchester United, and Italy's AC Milan and Juventus, are supported around the world. These teams are run as powerful businesses that generate millions of dollars per year. Their top players are often as famous—and as well paid—as movie stars.

All over the world

From its official beginnings in Europe in the 1800s, soccer has spread to almost every part of the world. Historically South America and Europe—where the game is known as "football"—have been soccer's powerhouses. However, the rise of women's soccer in the U.S. and the emergence of great players and teams from nations in Africa, Asia, Australasia, and the Middle East have turned the game into a truly global sport.

From Earliest Beginnings

Soccer has ancient origins. More than 2,000 years ago, Chinese, Japanese, Greek, and Roman cultures all featured games that involved players kicking or carrying a ball through a goal. Later, in the Middle Ages, violent contests between two teams of unlimited numbers were often played in the streets of towns and villages. A pig's bladder or stuffed animal skin served as the ball. In the 1800s soccer became organized with official rules. By the end of the century, it had evolved into more or less the game we play today.

▲ A pig's bladder is blown up for a game of pallo. Played in Europe in the 1600s, it was an early version of soccer.

The Football Association

In 1863 representatives from 11 English "football" teams met at the Freemason's Tavern in London to form the Football Association (FA). Until then, the hundreds of schools and teams that played soccer each had their own set of rules. Some teams played by rules that allowed holding the ball or tripping, for example, while others did not. Out of this chaos the FA devised a single set of rules. Within a decade, the English FA was joined by FAs from Wales, Scotland, and Ireland. In 1882 these four created the International Football Association Board (IFAB), which attempted to rule and regulate soccer around the world.

▲ During the Victorian era the typical outfit for soccer teams, such as the Scottish international side of 1892 (above), included caps and knee breeches (long shorts).

▲ Dating from the 1500s, the annual Shrove Tuesday soccer game in the town of Ashbourne, England, has no referees and very few rules. The goals are placed at either end of the town and the teams are known as Up'ards and Down'ards.

◀ The Japanese game of kemari was developed from ball games played in Ancient China more than 2,000 years ago. In kemari players had to pass the ball to each other without it touching the ground.

Explosion in interest

Toward the end of the 1800s, soccer spread like wildfire around the globe, introduced first by British traders and sailors and then by travelers from other European nations. Between 1890–1910, dozens of countries, from Austria to Brazil and Hungary to Russia, formed their own soccer teams, competitions, and associations. In 1904, tired of the IFAB burying its head in the sand, the *Fédération Internationale de Football Association* (FIFA) was formed by France and six other European nations. Soccer was now a truly international sport.

◄▲ *Despite some opposition from the male-dominated establishment, women's soccer games grew in popularity from the 1880s onward.*

► *Until the 1940s, balls and shoes were made from heavy, unwaterproofed leather. On a wet field, both ball and shoes would get much heavier and lose their shape.*

Early games and rules

Soccer games from the 1870s and 1880s onward attracted large crowds and much interest. Many of the basic rules of the game were in place by then. Modifications to the game, such as two-handed throw-ins and penalty kicks, were introduced. For a long time, goalkeepers could be charged at and knocked over at any time; later this was allowed only when they had the ball. However, goalies could use their hands on the ball anywhere on the field. This rule changed after a flood of goals were scored in 1910 by goalkeepers throwing the ball into the opposition's net!

▲ *Shinguards were invented in 1874 by Samuel W. Widdowson, a player for the English team Nottingham Forest, and who also played for England in 1880.*

► *The England shirt (right) was worn in the first official international game, which was against Scotland in 1872. Before this date caps were used to distinguish between teams. Caps then became keepsakes for playing for your country.*

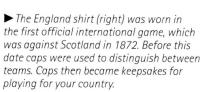

Field and Players

The field, or pitch, is where it all happens—where players pit their skills against each other and where games are won and lost. For professional games there are two teams of 11 players on a field 110–120 yards long and 70–80 yards wide. These teams play two 45-minute halves, plus injury or stoppage time.

Goals are 8 feet high and 24 feet wide. Corner flags are at least 5 feet tall to protect players from injury.

The penalty spot is a circle marked out 12 yards from the goal line

Center spot—the place where a kickoff restarts the game, either after a goal or at the beginning of each half

Sideline (Touchline)

Center circle—at kickoffs, opponents cannot enter this circle until the ball has been played

Field dimensions

Although professional fields usually are the standard 110 yards by 77 yards, a legal field can be anywhere between 100–130 yards long and 50–100 yards wide.

Player positions

Soccer started off simply with players being either forwards or backs. Now with sweepers, midfield anchors, wingers, and target men, player positions have become more complicated. That said, outfield players tend to be grouped into three categories—defenders, midfielders, and attackers. Players' shirts are numbered to aid identification, and ever since the 1920s, teams have been asked to change into a second, or away, shirt if their colors clash with those of the home side.

◀ Melbourne City players wear their team's new home (left) and away (right) shirts for 2014–2015. Many teams have two or three shirts and change the shirt, short, and sock design every season.

Ball in play

Ball in play

Ball out of play

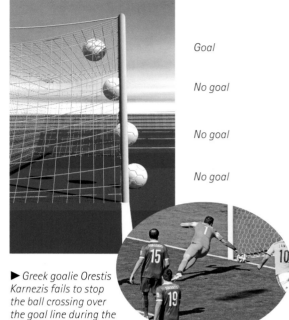

Goal

No goal

No goal

No goal

▶ *Greek goalie Orestis Karnezis fails to stop the ball crossing over the goal line during the 2014 FIFA World Cup.*

In or out?

The ball is only out of play when it completely crosses the boundary lines of the field—including the goal line. A throw-in, goal kick, corner kick, or goal is awarded depending on where the ball went out and which side touched it last. This applies to a ball in the air as well as one on the ground—so a clearance that curves over the sideline before landing in play will result in a throw-in to the opposition.

Midfield line—divides the field into two equal areas of play. Players have to stay in their own half before a kickoff

Penalty arc—during a penalty kick, only the penalty taker is allowed in this space

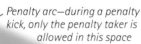

Corner arc—corner kicks must be taken inside this area

▲ *Red Bull Salzburg's stadium was the only one in Austria's top division to have a field made from artificial turf. It was re-covered in grass for use at the 2008 European Championships.*

Penalty area—known as "the box" and the area in which a goalie is allowed to handle the ball. Commit a foul in your box and your team could be facing a penalty

Goal line (Endline)— if the ball completely crosses this line, a goal kick, corner, or goal will be awarded

Goal area—known as the "six-yard box" and the area in which goal kicks must be taken

▼ *Norwegian groundsmen sweep the snow prior to a Tromso, Norway, game.*

▲ *This 1995 game between Wimbledon and Blackburn Rovers (both of England) was played in a mudbath at Selhurst Park stadium.*

The field

The rise of artificial turf in North America, and in stadiums all over the world prompted ex-England manager Terry Venables to cowrite a book entitled *They Used To Play On Grass*. Yet a new century still sees grass as king, even though it requires a lot of care and preparation. A stadium's groundstaff is responsible for getting a field ready for the game. Technical advances, such as soil management and undersoil heating, have helped reduce the number of games called off due to bad weather in many countries around the world.

See also

14-15 Fouls and Misconduct

54-55 Free Kicks

64-65 Tactics

▲ A referee's signals communicate clearly to everyone watching: a direct free kick (top left), an indirect free kick (above), or a red card for a player to leave the field (left).

Key Rules

Knowing the laws of the game is not only part of becoming a soccer player, it can also give you the edge in games. If you break the rules, you may forfeit your hard-earned possession of the ball to your team's disadvantage.

Guardians of the game

Players should observe all the rules on the field, but in practice it falls on the shoulders of the referee and his assistants to enforce the laws of the game. The officials make judgments on offsides, fouls, and misconduct (see pages 14–15), whether the ball was in or out of play, and if a hand ball has occurred. They have a range of signals at their disposal to communicate their decision to other officials, players, and spectators.

▲ A corner kick is signaled clearly by the referee pointing to the corner flag.

▼ This referee is signaling for a goal kick to be taken from the goal area.

◀ The referee's assistant reinforces the referee's goal-kick signal by pointing his flag level with the front edge of the goal area.

▼ There are two stages to the signals for offside. First, the referee's assistant raises his flag upright to indicate that an offside has occurred. Following this, he angles his flag to show whether the offside occurred on the far side (1), center (2), or near side (3) of the field.

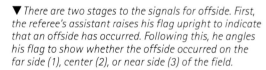

▲ The assistant signals a throw-in, pointing a flag at the goal that the throwing-in team is attacking.

◀ The assistant signals for a corner and checks that the ball is placed within the corner arc by the kicker.

▲ The assistant signals that a substitution is about to take place.

Advantage rule

Referees have some flexibility in how they interpret the rules. A key part of this flexibility is the advantage rule. Playing advantage means that the referee has spotted a foul or infringement, but instead of awarding a free kick, he lets the game continue because it offers an advantage to the side sinned against. A good example of this is when an attacker is fouled but still manages to pass to a teammate. The advantage rule reduces the number of interruptions and helps keep the game flowing.

▲ Video Assistant Referees (VAR) have been in use in several major leagues since 2018. Goals, penalties, red cards, and mistaken identity can result in a VAR review (above), but the referee still has the final say on any decision.

Offside

More controversy is generated by Law 11 than any other. The offside law has been altered over the years to help create attacking and counterattacking play. Most of the offside rule's bad press comes from its apparent complexity, yet the basic gist of the law is simple:

A player is offside if he is involved in active play and—at the moment the ball is played forward by a teammate—he is closer to the opposition's goal line than both the ball and the second-from-last opponent.

A player cannot be offside in his own half of the field or when receiving the ball direct from a goal kick, corner, or throw-in.

Examine these words. Opponents include the goalie as well as outfield players, so if you're level with the second-from-last opposition player, you are not offside. The "at the moment the ball is played" part is vital, too. An essential part of attacking is to time your runs so that you're onside as the ball is played ahead of you, yet can be behind defenders to collect the ball moments later. Being "involved in active play" can be hard to judge, but it usually means playing or touching the ball, being in a position to distract an opponent or prevent them from playing, or gaining an advantage from being offside (by scoring from a rebound, for example).

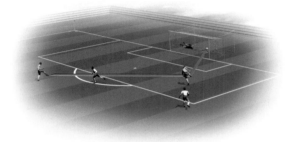

▲ When the ball was played is absolutely vital in an offside decision. Here the player who scores is clearly in an offside position when the ball is played. His "goal" is therefore disallowed as a result.

▲ The first attacker has foiled the onrushing goalkeeper by slipping the ball to a teammate. With two defenders between the goalscorer and the goal, the player is onside, and the goal is allowed.

▲ Referees must judge if a player is involved in active play when offside. The player top left is offside, but is not considered to be actively involved with play. The player who shoots is onside when he scores, and the goal is counted.

▲ You cannot be offside if you're behind the ball at the moment it is played. The scoring attacker only has the goalie in front of him. Yet he is not offside because the ball was cut back to him by his teammate.

Fouls and Misconduct

Act against the spirit of the game or break its laws at your own risk. It's the referee's job to penalize actions such as shirtpulling or tripping a player. If the offense is serious enough, you may be cautioned or even sent off the field.

See also

12-13 Key Rules

54-55 Free Kicks

58-59 Penalty!

Foul!

Tripping, pushing, or holding back an opponent are just a few of the offenses that are considered fouls. Depending on the offense and where it took place, the fouled-against team will be awarded a direct free kick, indirect free kick, or penalty. Some free-kick offenses, such as attempting to kick an opponent, apply even if the player fails to make contact. Offenses resulting in an indirect free kick include time-wasting and obstruction. For a complete list of fouls, look at a copy of the laws of the game.

No.1 Bobby Charlton

Some of the world's greatest footballers have also been the most well behaved. During a career spanning more than 20 years and 860 team and country appearances, English soccer player Bobby Charlton was never sent off the field.

▼ *France's Zinedine Zidane shocked the world with a head butt to the chest of Marco Materazzi during the final of the 2006 World Cup.*

MASTERCLASS
Fouls and misconduct

Never argue with a referee. The referee's decision is final.

Never retaliate if you've been fouled. This is also a punishable offense.

Channel your aggression into winning the game, not attacking your opponents.

Always keep your cool and trust the officials to uphold the laws of the game.

▶ *Switzerland's Ramona Bachman has her shirt pulled by Canadian defender Lauren Sesselmann during the 2015 Women's World Cup. Shirt pulling is just one of many fouls that can result in a free kick or penalty, and the offending player may be shown a yellow or a red card.*

▼ *Spain's Xabi Alonso is guilty of dangerous play as he goes in high on Iraq's Hawar Mulla Mohammed.*

Booking

A booking, also known as a yellow card or a caution, sees the referee holding up a yellow card and the player's name and shirt number being written down in the ref's book. Misconduct, including cynical, deliberate, and dangerous play, is likely to make the referee reach for the yellow card. Players can also be booked for persistent minor infringements or for removing their shirt to celebrate a goal.

Don't see red

Tempers often run high on the field, but that's no excuse for fighting or shouting. If you're guilty of any of these offenses, or if you prevent a clear goal-scoring opportunity by fouling or handling the ball, you can expect a red card. Two yellow-card offenses also equal a red card. The red card is no badge of honor. Players who have been given their marching orders let their team down and give the opposition a big advantage. Being sent off can also result in a player being banned from playing in one or more games.

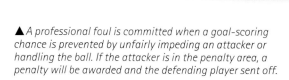

▲ *A professional foul is committed when a goal-scoring chance is prevented by unfairly impeding an attacker or handling the ball. If the attacker is in the penalty area, a penalty will be awarded and the defending player sent off.*

Under pressure

Refereeing is a tough job. Referees and assistants have to judge a fast-moving, dynamic game for 90 minutes or more. Officials are only human and do make occasional mistakes. With the recent addition of Video Assistant Referees (VAR), referees have a chance to correct any errors of judgment by watching incidents from the game on a pitch-side screen. The referee's decision is always final.

▼ *Italy's Pierluigi Collina was one of the world's top referees until he retired in 2005. He never shied away from tough decisions.*

SUISSE

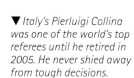

RED-CARD OFFENSES

A second cautionable offense

Using foul and abusive language

A professional foul

Violent conduct

Serious foul play such as deliberate hand ball

▼ *Officials can be subjected to verbal abuse and sometimes worse from a hostile crowd. Here, riot police use their shields to protect the referee after the crowd turned ugly during the Venezuela vs. Uruguay qualifying match for the 2014 FIFA World Cup.*

See also

10-11 Field and Players

60-61 Managers and Coaches

68-69 A Pro's Life

▲ This warm-up move involves performing a series of vigorous jumping jacks to get the blood circulating.

▲ Run and skip with an exaggerated high knee action, using your arms for balance.

▲ This exercise involves jogging along with a high backlift so that your heels almost touch your rear.

Ready to Play

With seconds to go before the ref blows the whistle and the game starts, the tension is mounting. Are you ready for the game—really ready? Have you stretched and warmed up properly? Is your uniform clean and have you had enough water?

Warm-up act

Being prepared for a game involves much more than packing a spare set of socks, crossing your fingers, and jogging out onto the field. Players of all ages and abilities need to warm up and get their bodies ready for the game. Warming up can involve activities such as jogging round the field, some short sprints, jumping jacks, and other routines. Teams that have warmed up properly may have an advantage over their opponents, allowing them to react more quickly in the opening minutes.

Stretching

Soccer can push your body to the limit, and stretching the muscles before a match allows them to perform at their peak, improving performance and reducing injuries. Warm up before stretching, and always ease gently into and out of a stretch—never stretch too far. Hold each stretch position for five to ten seconds, and repeat the stretch several times.

▼ Perform this thigh stretch after the other stretches. Using one hand for support, pull back your leg smoothly. Hold for ten seconds and then repeat with the other leg.

▲ To perform a side stretch, start with your feet about shoulder-width apart. Bend smoothly to one side as far as possible, letting your arm trail down your leg. Hold and then repeat, bending to the other side.

▲ For floor splits, push your head down toward each knee and the ground, holding for five seconds.

▲ Sitting down with the soles of your feet pressed together, use your elbows to push your knees down and hold the position to stretch your groin muscles.

◀ Like all professional players, Luka Modric, here playing for Croatia, warms up and stretches thoroughly before practice or a game.

▼▶ *Some shoes like those below used in an MLS game feature cleats molded into the sole of the shoe. Many shoes come with replaceable, screw-in cleats (right).*

Walk a mile in my shoes

First and foremost, your shoes must be a comfortable fit. Don't squeeze your foot into a size too small or let it float around in a size too large just because it's endorsed by your favorite player. Agüero, Messi, or Ronaldo's footwear isn't going to transform you into these heroes. Forget the logos and the hype—a pair of shoes that fits well, and is well made and looked after is all that you need.

Good shoes are made of soft leather to let your foot "feel" the ball—regular cleaning and polishing will help keep the leather soft. Good shoes are also flexible, should offer you plenty of support around the ankle, and have a wide tongue that won't slip to one side or the other. When your shoes get wet, allow them to dry naturally instead of in front of a heat source, otherwise the leather might crack. Help them keep their shape by stuffing them with newspaper after wear.

▲ *Shinguards are required at all levels of the modern game. Get used to shinguards by wearing them during practice and practice games.*

Shirts, shorts, and shinguards

Cotton shirts and shorts have been largely replaced by artificial materials. Tucking your shirt into your shorts isn't just about looking neat—it gives opponents less material to grab. Socks can be held up with small strips of material called ties. In earlier times sliding newspapers down the front of your socks was the only protection against a crack across the shins. Today's shinguards are usually made of plastic, but can prevent you from getting bruised.

◀ *Unlike early soccer balls, today's balls are lightweight and waterproof, like this Adidas Brazuca (top) used in the 2014 World Cup.*

▲ *The heavy cotton shirts of the past (left) have largely been replaced by clothing manufactured from lighter artificial materials (right).*

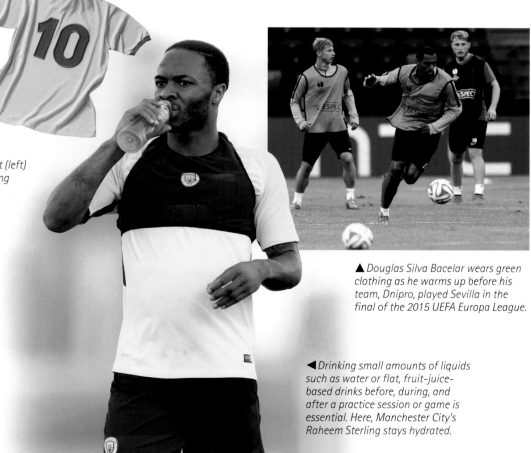

▲ *Douglas Silva Bacelar wears green clothing as he warms up before his team, Dnipro, played Sevilla in the final of the 2015 UEFA Europa League.*

◀ *Drinking small amounts of liquids such as water or flat, fruit-juice-based drinks before, during, and after a practice session or game is essential. Here, Manchester City's Raheem Sterling stays hydrated.*

MASTERCLASS
Ready to play

Take warming up seriously, even if teammates don't.

Remember to ease your way gently through a stretch.

Clean and look after your uniform. It will last longer that way.

Wear a sweatsuit before a game to keep warm, and regularly drink small amounts of water.

See also

24–25 Movement and Space

36–37 Fancy Skills

44–45 Opening Up Defenses

◄ For inside- or outside-foot cushioning, get into position early with your weight on your supporting leg. Watch the ball until it contacts your foot, then bring your foot back slightly to pull the ball down.

▲ Use the underside of your foot to trap the ball. Bring your foot down firmly, but don't stamp on the ball—it may pop out from under your control.

Ball Control

A long ball from a teammate is coming your way. Although you could just alter its direction with a touch of your foot, most of the time you'll want to slow the ball down and get it at your feet, ready for a run, pass, or a shot at goal. Welcome to ball control—one of the game's most essential groups of skills.

The soft option

"Damping" and "killing" are terms often used to describe stopping the speed (pace) and direction of a ball. What you're actually doing is cushioning the ball. This involves following the direction of the ball with the part of your body that makes contact with it. Whichever part of your body you use for cushioning, try to stay relaxed and balanced, watch the ball very closely, and move as smoothly as possible.

▲ Liverpool's Brazilian attacking midfielder Roberto Firmino is perfectly balanced as he prepares to cushion the ball using the inside of his foot.

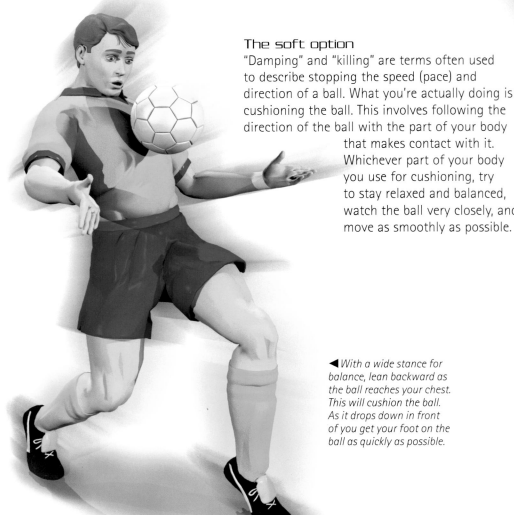

◄ With a wide stance for balance, lean backward as the ball reaches your chest. This will cushion the ball. As it drops down in front of you get your foot on the ball as quickly as possible.

No.2 Ruud Gullit

The Dutch player Ruud Gullit was a superb controller of the ball. He had a wonderful first touch, which gave him plenty of time and room to deploy his other formidable skills.

Control surfaces

Almost any part of your body that's allowed to touch the ball according to the rules can be used to get the ball under control. Your thigh and the top, or instep, of your foot are two of the more difficult parts to use, but are very effective when a ball falling steeply and sharply in front of you. Whichever area of the body you choose, try to use your arms to keep yourself balanced and aligned with the ball.

"Once you can control the ball, football [soccer] becomes a simple game."

Ferenc Puskás, former Hungarian captain

▲ *The instep cushion requires you to get your foot up, with the instep facing the ball and the toe pointing slightly down. As the ball arrives bring your foot down with the ball resting just above it.*

MASTERCLASS
Ball control

Watch the incoming ball like a hawk.

Get into position as early as you can, and try to keep your body relaxed.

Just before impact move the cushioning part of your body in the direction of the ball's flight.

Try to set the ball down as close as possible to your feet.

▶ *For the thigh cushion, the upper part of your leg should be almost parallel with the ground. Then pull your leg down and back as the ball makes contact. This will kill the ball's speed and should leave it in front of you.*

Practice, practice, practice

Don't wait until your side's next practice session—get out there and practise your ball-control skills whenever you can. Work with a friend and pass the ball to each other at different speeds and heights. On your own? No problem. Find an outside wall in a safe place and bounce a ball off it at varying angles to practise the full range of cushioning skills.

▲ Pinpoint sidefoot passes can be made on the move, as Fulham's Margunn Haugenes shows.

Passing

Passing glues together a team's play, turns defense into attack, switches the direction of play, and creates goal-scoring opportunities. When you make a pass, you have to decide where and to whom you are passing, when to release the ball, and which type of pass to make.

Accuracy and weight

Accuracy is the key to good passing. The ball needs to travel in the direction that you want without it being intercepted by the opposition. Your pass also needs to reach its destination in a way that makes it easy for the receiver to control. An important factor is the speed with which the ball leaves your foot. This is also known as the weight of a pass, and it varies depending on how far back you take your kicking foot and how fast you bring your foot through the ball. Only experience teaches you how to vary the weight of a pass.

"I was right-footed to start with, but I worked harder on my left, and it became better than my right."

George Best

◄ England captain Harry Kane has the ball under control at his feet, ready to make a pass or run with the ball.

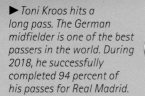

▶ Toni Kroos hits a long pass. The German midfielder is one of the best passers in the world. During 2018, he successfully completed 94 percent of his passes for Real Madrid.

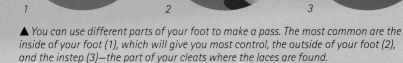

▲ You can use different parts of your foot to make a pass. The most common are the inside of your foot (1), which will give you most control, the outside of your foot (2), and the instep (3)—the part of your cleats where the laces are found.

1 *2* *3*

▲ *Striking the middle of the ball with a smooth follow-through keeps the ball low as it travels over the field. This makes it easier for a teammate to receive and control. Sidefoot passes are especially useful up to distances of approximately 65 feet.*

Sidefoot passing

The sidefoot pass, or push pass, uses the inside of the foot to strike the ball, keeping it close to the ground. You'll feel in control with this pass because a large portion of the foot makes contact with the ball, making it easier to direct the ball precisely where you want it. Your nonkicking foot should be close to the ball and point in the direction of the pass. With your body over the ball and your eyes focused on it, swing your leg from your hip through the ball. Keep your ankle firm as you make impact, and aim to hit the ball through its center.

▲ *Manchester's David Silva makes a textbook sidefoot pass. His kicking foot follows through to point at the target.*

No.3 Kevin de Bruyne

Manchester City and Belgium's Kevin de Bruyne has been described as a "complete midfielder" thanks to his superb passing, his goals, and his crucial interceptions.

▼ *Place two cones or other objects 20–30 inches apart. Pass the ball between the cones. Gradually stand farther away and shrink the distance between the cones to work on passing accuracy.*

Passing drill

Top soccer players never give up honing their passing skills. Take passing practices as seriously as the professionals. Aim for quick control and crisp, accurate passes to the receiver. The biggest single improvement you can bring to your game is to become a fully two-footed player. To do this, you'll need to work especially hard on your weaker foot in practices. Ask your coach for a range of different passing drills so that you don't get bored performing the same exercises every time you practice.

MASTERCLASS
Passing

Keep your head still and your eyes focused on the ball as you make the pass.

Aim to strike the ball with the correct amount of weight.

Move as soon as you've made the pass.

Build up passing skills with your weaker foot and practise as often as possible.

See also

20-21 Passing

26-27 On-ball Skills

36-37 Fancy Skills

Advanced Passing

Players with a wide range of different passing techniques at their disposal often control and dictate a game. While the sidefoot pass is the most frequently used, other passing techniques allow you to hit a bouncing ball, to chip the ball, or to make very long passes.

No.4 Andrea Pirlo

Italian World Cup winner Andrea Pirlo's range of passing was matched by his awareness on the field. With these skills he made his team tick by controling play and possession of the ball.

◀ *When under pressure, select a target and type of pass that you can execute accurately and quickly. Here the player hits a sidefoot pass.*

▲ *A chip pass will carry the ball over the heads of your opponents. Aim to strike the bottom of the ball with a downward stab and a short follow-through. Your foot and the ground act as a wedge, forcing the ball up at a steep angle.*

Timing

If the player you're passing to is on the move, you'll need to calculate where this teammate will be when the pass reaches his or her feet. Aim for this spot, not where your teammate is positioned when you strike the ball. Even with a relatively short pass, the player receiving the ball might have run forward several feet.

◄ The compass drill is a good way of sharpening your passing skills. As the ball is passed a player shouts north, south, east, or west. The player in the center then has to turn and pass the ball in that direction.

Instep drive

The instep pass, or drive, allows you to hit longer passes when you're standing still or on the move. With arms out for balance, nonkicking foot next to the ball, and your body over the ball, swing your kicking leg back then forward with your toes pointing at the ground. Your shoelaces should make contact with the middle of the ball. The follow-through should be long and smooth. By changing the angle of your foot and body, as well as the length of your backswing, you can make passes of different heights and lengths.

► Norwegian midfielder Alex Tettey hits a lofted instep drive. His body is upright and the follow-through takes his kicking leg across his body.

▲ A lofted instep drive will take the ball quickly through the air. To make this kind of pass, plant the nonkicking foot behind and to the side of the ball. You'll need to strike the lower half of the ball, and on the follow-through your leg should swing across your body.

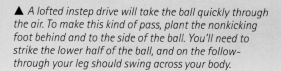
"Football [soccer] is a simple game based on the giving and taking of passes." Bill Shankly

Flick passes

You'll often receive the ball under great pressure, with opponents closing in on you. Inside and outside flick passes are ideal when time and space is limited. Flicks are short passes along or just above the ground. Use the toe end of your shoe in a short but firm flicking movement. If you're under extreme pressure, you can also use your toe and lower laces of your instep to flick the ball right back to the player who has just passed the ball to you.

MASTERCLASS
Advanced passing

Use the instep drive for longer passing.

Try to keep your body between opponents and the ball as you release a pass.

When making shorter passes, especially in crowded areas, use the sidefoot pass

◄ In tight situations such as this you can use the outside of your foot to perform a flick pass. Try to make contact with the ball, using the little toe area of your cleats.

See also

20–21 Passing

26–27 On-ball Skills

42–43 Attacking Skills

Movement and Space

Movement and awareness of available space are vital components of any good passing team and will allow you to let the ball do the work. Crisp, accurate passing combined with decisive movements can get the ball around a field faster than a single player or covering defenders can travel. Precise passing and movement can open up even the tightest of defenses.

▲ Practice passing in triangles, with players interchanging positions, yet keeping relatively close to each other (less than 32–40 feet apart) as they move around the field.

▲ Mark out an area with cones. Three players should try to keep possession of the ball from a defender by passing and moving. If the defender gets the ball or it goes out of play, he or she should switch places with one of the other three.

MASTERCLASS
Movement and space

With or without the ball, always keep your head up, looking for opportunities to move into space.

Be aware of the positions of opponents, teammates, and the player with the ball.

Soccer is fast. Space that was there the last time you looked may have gone. Other space may have opened up elsewhere. Check first.

No.5 Enzo Scifo

Belgian legend Enzo Scifo was both masterful at passing and excellent at support play, seemingly able always to find good positions in which to receive the ball.

Be a space invader

The soccer field is a big place. Even with a full set of players, pockets of clear space still exist. It's these that you should be looking for and moving into. Not having the ball is no reason to relax—just the opposite in fact. Use the time to search for an open space in a good position, invade the space, and look to receive a pass. Soccer is a dynamic game with opportunities opening up or closing remarkably quickly. Look not just for space but areas that aren't blocked off by defenders—positions that offer the on-ball player a clear, safe path to pass to you.

▼ The "push and go" sees a player pass the ball beyond a defender and then run on to collect it quickly. Start sprinting as soon as the ball leaves your foot.

Pass and move

Don't rest on your laurels and stand still after delivering a pass. Get moving and look to support the player who now has the ball. Alert players seek to get themselves quickly into a position to receive the ball again or into clear space for the second, third, or fourth pass in a move. By acting quickly after making a pass, you can catch defenders off guard and open up play.

Slipping markers

A player looking to receive the ball must sometimes shake off a defender who is marking him closely. Jogging around aimlessly won't help your team. Make life hard for the defender with sudden changes of speed or direction—fake a move away from your target space, then turn quickly, and sprint into it to trick a marker.

▲ For the wall pass, approach the defender, wait until he closes in on you, then exchange sidefoot passes with a teammate who plays the ball into available space.

Space behind opponents

A key area to exploit is the space behind a nearby opponent, so be on the lookout. The opponent is guarding an area of the field, so getting past him can open up opportunities. Dribbling and turning (see On-ball Skills, pages 26–27) can get you past, but so can other, less-fancy techniques. One move is the wall, or return pass, where you pass to a teammate then receive it straight back on the other side of a defender. Another is the more risky push-and-go, where you approach a defender, push the ball past him to one side, and run on to collect it. The defender has to turn while you're heading the right way.

▲ Inside hook. Lean into the direction you want to turn and hook the inside of your foot right around the ball, dragging it with you as you turn and move away.

Turning

Changing direction with the ball is an important part of your game. In busy areas of the field, look to turn and change direction as soon as you receive a pass and have the ball under control. This often outwits opponents and buys you precious time to look up and make a pass or shot, or set out on a run. Always keep yourself between the ball and opponents when making a turn, and swivel on one foot, using the other to move the ball either with sidefoot or instep nudges, if you have enough room, or by using an outside or inside hook, if under pressure.

◄ Senegal's Sadio Mané holds off Juan Cuadrado of Colombia, ready to move sharply away and into clear space.

▲ Outside hook. Leaning in the direction you want to turn, reach across your body with that side's foot. Hook the outside of your foot around the ball, and sweep it away as you turn.

See also

20-21 Passing

22-23 Advanced Passing

42-43 Attacking Skills

On-ball Skills

Running with the ball, protecting it from opponents, and dribbling are all skills that require good ball control and excellent awareness of the game around you.

◄ French star Franck Ribéry shows good balance as he sprints forward with the ball under control.

Moving with the ball

If you have the ball and see a large, promising area of open space ahead, move into it as quickly as possible. You must kick the ball far enough to allow you to maintain a good running speed but not so far that you lose control and—even worse—possession of the ball. Using the outside of the foot allows you to keep moving at good speed. When running with the ball, you need to have eyes everywhere, so keep glancing up at the game around you while staying aware of the position of the ball.

▲ Shielding requires some strength, but mostly you need skill and an ability to watch out for opponents.

▲ This player has the ball under control and has turned his body to shield the ball from his opponent.

◄ Arsenal's Alexandre Lacazette keeps his body between the ball and Leicester City's Jonny Evans, displaying strong shielding skills.

▲ The player now has a little more time to choose his next move, which is a lay-off sidefoot pass.

Shielding

Shielding, or screening, is a way to keep control of the ball and prevent opponents from stealing possession. You put your body between an opponent and the ball and keep it there legally, even if that means shifting position as your opponent moves. The difference between shielding the ball and impeding another player largely comes down to whether you have the ball under control. You cannot just block the path of an opponent or push or hold onto him. As soon as you start shielding, keep the ball under control and think about your next step. This is most likely to be a pass to an unmarked teammate, although it can be a much fancier move, such as a hook and turn (see page 25).

MASTERCLASS
On-ball skills

Good balance, shielding, and awareness are needed when you have the ball.

Think about the result of your on-ball move—where, when, and to whom are you going to pass?

One-on-one drills and small-sided games are the places to hone your on-ball skills.

Always look for the simple option.

▲ The player running and dribbling the ball is about to be closed down by a defender. The dribbler drops his right shoulder and leans a little in one direction.

Dribbling

A skill guaranteed to get crowds on their feet, dribbling calls for good balance, superb control, and plenty of confidence. Keep the ball in front of you and close to your feet, but never under them or you may overrun the ball. You can use your instep and the outside and inside of your foot to nudge the ball forward and to each side. Dribbling is a high-risk move, and even the very best players surrender the ball on occasion. This is why you should only dribble when away from your defensive-third of the field, and always be on the lookout for a safe pass. A good dribbler knows where he is heading, and when to release the ball, and how to avoid getting cornered by two or three defenders.

▲ *Practice dribbling at walking pace, then build up your speed. Using slalom courses can help you keep your balance and control while changing direction.*

Dribbling deception

Unless you're blessed with outstanding speed, dribbling without deception is a surefire way of losing the ball. Deception can take the form of tricks such as feinting—pretending to move past an opponent in one direction, only to go the other way—or sudden changes in speed, from sprint to walk to sprint again. Feinting requires exaggeration and confidence to really convince the defender that you will head left, when you intend to go right. In all deception moves accelerate away from the opponent you have just deceived, keeping yourself between the ball and the player as much as possible.

▲ *For this dribble-and-tag game, each player is given a ball and must stay within the center circle. If you touch a player with your hand, you gain a point. If you are tagged, you lose a point; and if you lose control of the ball or dribble outside the circle, you forfeit two points.*

No.6 Eden Hazard

Belgian winger Eden Hazard is one of the world's best high-speed dribblers. His fast runs draw defenders toward him, allowing him to slip the ball to a teammate in space.

▲ *The body movement by the dribbler tricks the defender into believing his opponent is going to head one way. The defender follows through in that direction.*

▲ *As the defender follows through in the wrong direction the on-ball player is able to swerve around his opponent in the opposite direction and dribble away.*

See also

46–47 Defending

48–49 Defending as a Unit

1

2

3

4

▲ *For the front block tackle, the tackler (in white) approaches the on-ball player (1), getting his bodyweight over his foot and striking the ball firmly (2). The tackler concentrates on dispossessing his opponent (3) before moving away quickly with the ball under control (4).*

Tackling

When the opposition has the ball, there are a number of ways to win it back. You can try to intercept a pass or you can challenge the opponent with a tackle. Although tackling can leave you open to being dribbled around, it is a key part of the game. Tackling isn't just for defenders, it's a skill required all over the field.

▼ *This ill-timed lunge from behind doesn't make contact with the ball, and so it is a foul. The player may be booked or sent off, and a free kick or penalty will be awarded to the opposition depending on where the foul was committed.*

▶ *Real Madrid's Sergio Ramos times a strong sliding tackle to try to rob Liverpool's Fabio Borini during a 2014–2015 UEFA Champions League game.*

▼ *Brazilian defender Gabriel, playing for Arsenal, times his tackle on Everton's Belgian striker Romelu Lukaku.*

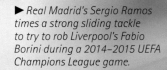
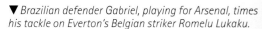

MASTERCLASS
Tackling

Always go for the ball, never the player.

During a tackle, watch the ball not your opponent.

Stand firm in block tackles, using your weight to make the tackle.

Once the tackle is made, get the ball under control, keep your head up, and start moving.

The front-block tackle

The block tackle is the most commonly used tackle. For this tackle, you'll usually be facing an opponent from the front. Plant your nontackling foot firmly on the ground and lean forward into the tackle. This will give you a solid base. Use the inside of your foot to make strong, firm contact with the middle of the ball. Often this will be enough to remove the ball from your opponent.

Tackling tips

The timing of a tackle really comes only with experience and practice. Try to make your move when your opponent is unbalanced, looking down at the ball, or playing it too far in front. Aim to tackle from the front or side, staying on your feet whenever possible. This enables you to steal the ball, or if you're unsuccessful in the tackle, to chase after the ball. Determination and confidence are very important—if you don't fully commit yourself to a tackle, your challenge is probably going to fail, and you are more likely to hurt yourself.

No.7 Franco Baresi

Franco Baresi, one of Italy's finest-ever sweepers, was a superb tackler. Along with Marco van Basten and Ruud Gullit he played a major role in AC Milan's successes.

▲ Sometimes players have to challenge when the ball is in midair. Here ex-Juventus player Paul Pogba (right) gets to the ball first in a match versus Olympique de Marseilles in 2015.

Sliding tackle

Sliding tackles are sometimes the only way to deflect or clear a ball. Although sliding tackles look spectacular, if they're executed badly there can be a high risk of injury or being penalized with a free kick or penalty. Make sure you bend your supporting leg at the knee as you slide in on it. As you make contact with the ball you need to transfer your bodyweight to your tackling leg and foot. Although they usually just clear the ball, some tacklers try to hook their foot around the ball to keep possession.

See also

36-37 Fancy Skills

42-43 Attacking Skills

44-45 Opening up Defenses

Volleying and Shooting

To get the ball past the goalkeeper and any defenders, your shot has to be struck with the right combination of power and accuracy. When the ball is off the ground, you'll need to make a volley. As well as attempts on goal, volleys can also be used for quick passes and long clearances.

No.8 Marco van Basten

Dutch center-forward Marco van Basten was a magnificent striker of the ball with some spectacular goals to his credit. These include a memorable volley against the U.S.S.R. in the 1988 European Championships.

The volley

A volley is made when the foot and ball connect in midair. Because you can get the full weight of your body into a volley, it's one of the most powerful shots you can make. When a volleyed shot comes off, it can be spectacular but you'll need to keep your eye on the ball and accurately judge its speed as it comes toward you.

1

2

3

▲ For a side volley, lean back a little from the incoming ball (1) and swing your leg up and around, making contact with your instep (2). Make sure your foot is over the ball to keep it down and follow through smoothly and firmly (3).

▲ Volleys can be used in defense as well as attack. Here, Italian defender Fabio Cannavaro performs a spectacular overhead volley to clear the ball away from his penalty area.

Sidefoot volleying

Using the side of your foot, you can perform two types of volley. The first is a gentle, slightly-cushioned pass to a nearby teammate who is in a better position. This is called a layoff volley. You'll need to meet the ball early and your foot should make contact with the middle, or just above the middle, of the ball. The sidefoot volley can also be used as a close-range shot to steer a bouncing ball toward the goal.

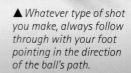

▲ Whatever type of shot you make, always follow through with your foot pointing in the direction of the ball's path.

1   2   3

◄ For a front-on instep volley, prepare to lift your knee and point your toes down (1). Keep your head in front of the knee of your kicking leg (2). Look for a clean contact to send the ball in the direction you want (3).

Shot placement

The instep drive is the basis of the shooting technique you'll most frequently use. Unlike using the instep for a long, lofted pass, the key to shooting is to get your body over the ball and to keep the shot low. If you have the time and space to pick an exact place to shoot, aim low into the corners of the goal. It takes a goalkeeper longer to dive low than to dive and stretch high. If you're at one side of the goal, try to aim for the corner of the goal not covered by the goalie.

MASTERCLASS
Volleying and shooting

Look to keep the ball low and on target.

Always follow up your shot or a teammate's in case of rebounds.

Commit yourself to a shot. Don't change your mind as you're about to shoot.

Don't be afraid—take a shot!

▲ For a half volley, the ball should be hit as soon as it touches the ground. Stretch your ankle so your toes point down and keep your knees bent.

► English legend Dixie Dean was famed for his incredibly powerful shooting. He scored 60 goals in a single season for Everton (1927–1928).

Shot selection

Long-range shots require a volley or instep drive to generate enough power to trouble the goalkeeper. If you have learned how to bend or swerve the ball, you'll be even more effective. From close range, many players prefer accuracy over power and hit the ball firmly with the sidefoot. If the goalkeeper has advanced off the goal line, a chip kick or lob may be the best shot to make.

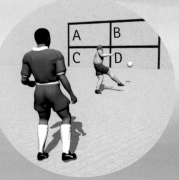
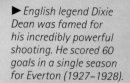
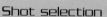

▲ Marked-out squares on a wall make excellent targets for shooting practice. One player passes the ball and calls out a square that the other player then attempts to hit.

▲ Germany's Thomas Müller (left) lobs the ball over the Cameroon goalkeeper during a 2014 friendly match.

Heading

A soccer ball can spend as much time in the air as on the field, so heading is a skill that all players—not just central defenders and strikers—need. Heading doesn't hurt—or rather, it shouldn't. Heading is painless as long as you use your forehead to make contact with the ball.

▲ *A power header from a running position involves a player leaping off his front foot to create maximum thrust as the ball is met. Bending the knees helps keep the player balanced on landing.*

▲ *Aim to hit the ball with your forehead. Remember to try to keep your eyes open until after contact.*

▲ *Corner kicks often create good heading opportunities. Excellent control is needed to guide the ball down and away from the goalie's hands.*

Eyes wide open

Usually when you make a header you'll be directing the ball horizontally or down. Try not to shut your eyes as you meet the ball, but watch it right onto your forehead. Your body position should allow you to get over the ball. The exception to this is when clearing a ball from defense. In this case, you still need to use your forehead, but position yourself underneath the ball to send it up and forward.

Meeting the ball

Only jump to head the ball when absolutely necessary. Heading with your feet on the ground gives you a more stable, balanced base. Try to get into position early and meet the ball, rather than just let the ball hit your head. You also need to keep your neck muscles taut just before you make contact in order to support your head and provide maximum control.

▶ *England striker Harry Kane attempts a spectacular diving header on Sweden's goal during the UEFA U21 European Championships in 2015.*

Power heading

To put more force into a header, arch your back and thrust your upper body and head forward and through the ball. For even more speed and distance you can spring off the ground to meet the ball in midair. Timing is essential. Ideally you want to connect with the ball at the top of your jump. You can generate extra force by driving your arms backward to help propel your head firmly through the ball.

No.9 Iván Zamorano

At a far-from-towering 5'10", Chilean striker Iván Zamorano proved for many years that you don't have to be the tallest player on the field to be an excellent header of the ball.

▲ *Belgian defender Vincent Kompany, here playing for Manchester City, makes a powerful defensive header upfield. Defenders with good heading ability such as Kompany are a threat in attack at corners or free kicks.*

▼ *Defensive headers require both height and distance. Here the defender meets the ball at the top of his jump and angles his head to clear a dangerous ball.*

Other headers

The cushioning header is similar to the basic header, but as the ball reaches your forehead you should recoil smoothly back and down, killing the speed of the ball and leaving it at your feet. The flick-on header tends to be used from a long clearance, a nearpost corner kick, or a goal kick from your goalie. Flick the ball behind you, hopefully in the direction of a strike partner. It is one of the most difficult headers to master.

▲ *This effective heading drill begins with one player using an underhand throw to lob the ball at headable height to a partner 15 feet away. The header should be aimed down toward the thrower's feet for him to practise ball control. After ten headers, swap positions.*

MASTERCLASS
Heading

Don't be scared of the ball.

Make sure your body is both balanced and relaxed.

If you can, keep your eyes open while heading the ball.

When jumping to head the ball, you can use your arms for balance, but keep your elbows down to avoid fouls or injuries.

See also

20-21 Passing

24-25 Movement and Space

30-31 Volleying and Shooting

Small-sided Games

Playing small-sided games is not only fun, it can also help improve your skills for regular games. Millions of people play small-sided games during their breaks from work, in fun after-school sessions, and in competitive evening and weekend divisions.

▲ Soccer players of all ages and skill levels can take part in and enjoy small-sided games, as these former stars playing in a veterans' five-on-five tournament, illustrate.

Why smaller games?

In games with 11 players on each side you may feel uninvolved and far from the action for long periods of the game. A big advantage of small-sided games is that they don't allow you to hide for long. Players see plenty of the ball, have to make more contact with the ball and playmaking decisions, and will practice certain skills and techniques more than they would in a regular game. There are also fewer stoppages and less reliance on set pieces. This forces players to be constantly prepared for action.

▼ ► Five-on-five has different rules to the regular game. Playing the ball over head height (right) and entering the goalie's area (below) are both banned.

Walled five-on-five

Five-on-five games allow players of all ages to compete in indoor or outdoor games, from informal lunchtime sessions to seriously contested divisions. Five-on-five rules vary, but usually ban the ball from traveling above shoulder or head height and ban outfield players from entering the goalkeeper's area. Many fields feature low-height goals, and walls instead of sidelines. These help keep the ball in play and encourage players to play passes off the walls to beat opponents.

► The walls surrounding five-on-five fields offer a handy way of beating opponents. Here the on-ball player's path to the left and straight ahead is blocked. He opts to play the ball against the wall, running around the other side of his opponent to collect it.

Small-sided games for young players

More and more youth and children's coaches are turning to small-sided games as a key way of developing young players' skills. Small-sided games place an emphasis on technique and movement, not height or physique, and so are ideal for players who are still growing. There aren't the large fields or strict team formations found in the full-sized game so everyone gets the chance to hone their attacking and defending skills. Small-sided games encourage attacking play. Players learn that a two or more goal deficit can be overcome quickly with fast, precise passing, movement, and low shots. The speed of the action also means there's no chance to worry about mistakes.

▲▶ Smaller fields and looser formations give youth players (above) and children playing in Jámy, the Czech Republic (right), greater opportunity to work on their skills.

Futsal

Futsal is a form of five-on-five soccer approved by FIFA in 1989 and increasingly played all over the world. There are no walls around the edge of the field, and the junior-sized ball can travel above head height. Played on a roughly basketball-sized court and with rolling substitutes, Futsal games have two 20-minutes halves, but the clock is stopped whenever the ball goes out of play. One rule states that if a team makes six serious fouls in one half, the ref will award a direct free kick no more than 40 feet from the goal, with no defensive wall allowed.

◀▲ Small-sided games can be played in a wide variety of locations. This inflatable court allows five-on-five action to spring up almost anywhere.

▲ A small-sided game of soccer is played in the La Boca area of Buenos Aires, Argentina, but there are similar sites in parks, backyards, and areas of open land all over the world. Players improve their skills with simple pickup games, playing keeping the ball up, or games of headers and volleys.

On the streets

Soccer can be played almost anywhere as long as it is away from traffic, windows, and other hazards. All top soccer players can fondly recall practising either on their own or with a few friends in the streets, backyards, and parks of their towns or cities. Many pros believe that their superb close skills came from kicking around a tennis ball or other small ball. The smaller ball demands excellent touch and close control.

Beach soccer

Beach soccer is a fun and popular pastime played by many that has recently grown into an organized sport. It features a number of prestigious tournaments, including the FIFA Beach World Cup. Brazil has been the most successful nation, winning the tournament 14 times, including the last competition in 2017.

◀▼ Russia's Artur Paporotnyi scores during the 2015 FIFA Beach Soccer World Cup. Brazilian maestro Zico (below) grew up playing beach soccer and other small-sided games which helped him develop his amazing skills.

"Football [soccer] is about glory . . . doing things in style . . . doing them with a flourish."

Danny Blanchflower

Fancy Skills

Spectacular overhead kicks, aerial side volleys, kicks from the halfway line—all breathtaking to watch, especially when executed by a Ronaldo or a Messi. You are more likely to make use of slightly less ambitious, but extremely valuable skills such as the back heel pass or dragback.

See also

30-31 Volleying and Shooting

34-35 Small-sided Games

◄ *The back heel is a good way of changing the direction of the ball and tricking your opponents. With your nonkicking foot level with the ball, strike through the center of the ball with your heel or the sole of your cleat.*

◄ *An aerial side volley is a spectacular way of dealing with a high, rising ball.*

Getting airborne

Overhead kicks can be made with one foot on or just off the ground and the ball hooked back over your head toward the goal. But the top-of-the-range bicycle kick will have you launching yourself off the ground and leaning far back as you swing your kicking foot back over your shoulder to hit the ball. Only ever try this on very soft ground or sand, never on artificial turf or a hard field.

Just for show

Skills such as the back heel and dragback are valuable techniques that can be used sparingly by all players. Other tricks, such as catching the ball on the back of your neck or the flick-up, are more for show and unlikely to be used during a game—but they can be fun to practice.

▲ *Lionel Messi strikes a spectacular overhead kick during a 2015 La Liga game. He gets his foot over the top of the ball to keep the ball's height down.*

► *For the flick-up, place one foot in front of the ball and trap it between the toes of your back foot and the heel of the front (1). Lift your back foot up to roll the ball over your heel (2), then flick the ball up (3) and over your head (4) so that it lands at your feet.*

1   2   3   4

▲ Mexico's Andrés Guardado nutmegs Argentina's Nicolás Otamendi during the 2010 FIFA World Cup.

You've been nutmegged

Few things are more embarrassing for a player than being nutmegged. A nutmeg means kicking the ball through the open legs of an opponent, either for a teammate to receive the pass on the other side or for you to run around the startled, nutmegged player and collect the ball. Nutmegs are risky, but when they work they can be effective.

1

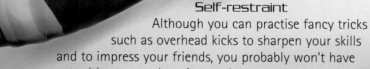

2

3

Self-restraint

Although you can practise fancy tricks such as overhead kicks to sharpen your skills and to impress your friends, you probably won't have many opportunities to use them in a real game. Only use these skills when it gives your team an advantage—rather than simply for the entertainment of other players and spectators.

No.10 Ronaldinho

Brazilian attacking midfielder Ronaldinho won three FIFA World Player of the Year awards. He dazzled both opponents and fans with his superb ball skills.

4

▼ Zinedine Zidane (below) displays great agility and skill to bring a high ball down with the inside of his foot while he is high in the air.

▲ The dragback is a way of catching an opponent off guard. You look as if you're going to play the ball in one direction, but instead you stop the ball (1), drag it back (2), and pivot (3) before heading off in another direction (4).

◄ Ivory Coast attacker Salomon Kalou balances a ball on his head during a practice session.

▲ Colombia's maverick goalkeeper René Higuita had a unique method of clearing the ball from his goal area. This technique, which involved flicking his feet over the back of his head, was dubbed the "scorpion kick."

▶ Real Madrid and Belgium goalkeeper Thibaut Courtois practices stopping or catching the ball at various heights and angles for many hours each week to hone his goalkeeping skills.

"The goalie has to be one of the fittest, most agile, quick-thinking, and determined players in the team." Gordon Banks

Goalkeeping Basics

Goalkeeping is a unique skill and one that holds a lot of responsibility. The only player allowed to handle the ball (inside his penalty area), a goalkeeper is the last line of defense. A sloppy goalkeeping performance can cause a strong side to lose a game, whereas an inspired performance can secure a memorable win. More hinges on the goalie than any other single player.

▲ Spanish keeper Iker Casillas displays a good stance, making any goalkeeping move possible.

Stance
Maintaining a good stance whenever the opposition is attacking is a straightforward yet vital part of goalkeeping. The basic stance is with the legs shoulder-width apart, the arms in front, head straight, and bodyweight slightly forward. Two of the most common mistakes are too wide a stance, which makes it hard to change direction, and staying flat-footed, which makes it almost impossible to move quickly. The goalie should be up on the balls of his feet whenever the ball is in a dangerous position.

▲ To gather in a ground-level ball, get down on one knee, get your hands behind the ball, and scoop it up with your knee and foot forming a barrier.

1

2

Hands are held with fingers pointing up to gather in a chest high ball (left). Courtois is forced to dive and stretch to save the ball traveling low and wide (right).

▲ *The above-head-height catch can be used to cut out high balls from the penalty area.*

Communication and positioning

Goalkeeping is all about preventing attacks from becoming goals, and many attacking chances can be snuffed out using nothing more spectacular than concentration, good basic positioning, and good communication. A well-placed and alert goalkeeper can often see the game in front of him better than his teammates and should relay advice to them. At set pieces, such as free kicks, the goalie should be in charge of his goal area. Instructions to players should be clear, brief, and calm.

Simple saves

Many shots and loose balls can be gathered in without resorting to a dive. The secret is quick footwork and a sharp eye to get in line with the incoming ball so that your body is fully behind the ball as you collect it. Try to cushion the ball on arrival. Goalkeepers do this by taking the ball early, giving them room to bring their hands back as the ball impacts, thus killing its speed. Remember: soft hands equal safe hands. Shots, loose crosses, stray passes, and knockdowns come at different heights, so goalies need to practice a range of ball-taking skills at waist, chest, ground, thigh, and head height.

▲ *With his arms 8–12 inches in front of his body, the goalie gets his hands behind and to the sides of the ball with his fingers spread out.*

MASTERCLASS
Goalkeeping basics

Maintain a good stance on the balls of your feet and with your head up, ready for action.

Get your body in line with an incoming ball, and always watch it all the way into your hands.

If you decide to go for a ball, shout loudly and be positive, determined, and decisive.

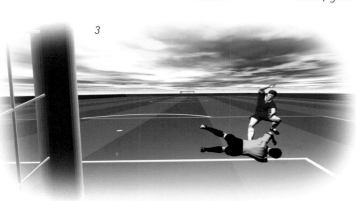

3

◀ *With the attacker clean through on goal, the goalie comes off his line to narrow the angle (1). Staying upright as long as possible (2), the goalie performs a smothering save, diving at the feet of the attacker, spreading himself out, and gathering in the ball (3).*

No.11 Gordon Banks

Gordon Banks was one of the finest goalies of his or any other era. Career highlights included a stunning save from Pelé in the 1970 World Cup and winning the 1966 World Cup with England.

See also

22–23 Advanced Passing | 38–39 Goalkeeping Basics

58–59 Penalty!

Goalkeeping Choices

The best goalkeepers are good communicators and know how to concentrate. A goalkeeper has to also make many decisions quickly and calmly throughout a game. A goalie has a number of different goal-stopping techniques to master, including punching the ball and diving saves. Dealing with back passes and distributing the ball to teammates are also essential skills.

MASTERCLASS
Goalkeeping choices

If a player in your half isn't free, kick a long ball upfield.

Good, clear communication can prevent many defensive errors.

Put any mistakes you make behind you, and concentrate on the rest of the game.

Remember the three B's of goalkeeping—be positive, be the boss, be first.

No.12 Dino Zoff

Italian goalkeeper Dino Zoff was a fine goalie and very calm under pressure. He once went a record 1,143 minutes without allowing a goal. He played at international level until the age of 41.

▶ *A dramatic leap to deflect the ball is sometimes the only way of preventing a goal. When tipping the ball over or around the goal, the goalkeeper must be alert for rebounds off the goal posts.*

Punch or deflect?

Although a two-handed catch is the ideal save to make, it's not always possible to get both hands fully on the ball. Sometimes punching or deflecting are the only options. To punch a ball, use both fists placed close together and angled slightly inward. With wrists firm aim to punch just below the middle of the ball with a short but strong jabbing action. On other occasions you'll be at full stretch and the only way of preventing a goal will be to deflect or tip the ball around the post or over the bar.

◀ *Girona's goalkeeper Yassine Bounou dives to stop Philippe Coutinho of Barcelona taking a shot on goal.*

Moving across the goal from the basic stance (1) this goalkeeper launches himself off one foot (2) and gets his hands behind the ball (3). He uses his body and arms to prevent the ball from popping out as he lands (4).

1   2   3   4

Diving

Every goalkeeper has to make diving saves. The ball should be caught in front of the body and always followed into the hands. Gather the ball in as quickly as possible to prevent it from bouncing out. One of the most difficult dives for a goalkeeper is the low drop onto the ball. To respond to a shot fired low and near to your body, push your legs away and get your body down and behind the ball.

Distribution

You've saved the ball—what now? You have to decide whether to distribute the ball either by foot or by hand. Throws tend to be more accurate, although kicking the ball, usually using an instep volley or half-volley, can cover more distance. There are three ways of throwing the ball: the underhand rollout, which is good for accuracy; the overhand throw for distance; and the javelin throw; where the ball is thrust forward using a bent arm. The javelin throw is often the quickest way of distributing the ball.

For an overhand throw, the arm should be kept relatively straight as it swings over with a bowling motion. A wide stance helps provide balance.

Former England goalkeeper Joe Hart performs an underarm throw. With his front foot and eyes pointing at his target, he releases the ball smoothly.

Joe Hart keeps his eyes on the ball as he distributes it up the field. He aims to strike the ball with his instep with plenty of power to send the ball a long distance up the field.

Backpass rule

The back pass rule was introduced to cut down on timewasting. The rule says that a throw-in or intentional pass back to the goalkeeper cannot be handled. If it is, an indirect free kick will be awarded to the other team. Don't try to be smart and attempt some fancy dribbling when the ball comes back to you. Hit a back pass cleanly and immediately, or if you have plenty of time and space, cushion and control the ball before launching it upfield. If you're under pressure, it's far better to give away a throw-in rather than a possible scoring chance.

French goalkeeper Hugo Lloris takes a long swing of his kicking foot to strike a goal kick a long way upfield.

See also

24-25 Movement and Space | 26-27 On-ball Skills | 20-21 Passing | 22-23 Advanced Passing

▲ As he approaches the defender the wide player with the ball passes to his teammate.

▲ With the defender indecisive, the wide player makes an overlapping run down the line.

▲ The wide player receives the return pass and now has time and space to make a cross or cut infield.

Attacking Skills

Attacking is not just the role of two or three forwards. Counterattacks are often started by defenders and driven forward by midfielders, while many crosses come from fullbacks out near the sideline. Every outfield player can take part in attacking moves and should develop the key skills involved.

Overloads and overlaps

Attacks that use plenty of a field's space, its width and depth, can stretch defenses and lead to goalscoring chances. Giving your attack depth means staggering your positions up the field. This not only allows the on-ball player to make a safe pass backward, it also makes it very difficult for a defender to set up and play the offside trap against you. Width is very important because the defense tends to concentrate in the middle of the field, and an overlapping run by a wide player down the touchline can lead to a great crossing opportunity. Always be on the lookout for an overload. An overload occurs when the attacking side has more players in the attacking third of the field than the defending side. This requires fast running and support from teammates.

▲ Giving your attack depth gives you more options. Here a pass has been made to the player on the far left who is making a late run into the area, staying onside and joining the attack at the last minute.

"Football [soccer] should always be played beautifully; you should play in an attacking way; it must be a spectacle." Johan Cruyff

MASTERCLASS
Attacking skills

Always look to support an attacking teammate with the ball, offering him passing and laying-off options.

Aim to cross the ball with accuracy and speed—don't just punt the ball into the area.

Split up into groups of defenders and attackers when practising attacking moves during practice.

Opening up spaces

Sometimes attackers break away from a defender or find space to receive the ball. On other occasions they move to create space for others to exploit. Attacking without the ball is very important, and it often involves an attacker making a quick change of direction or speed to take a defender with him. As the defender moves to cover his opponent, space that another attacker can run into appears.

▲ *A diagonal run across and into a defense, as done by the player in yellow on the left, can cause hesitancy among defenders. They may be unsure whether to follow him, opening up space for another attacker, or to leave him be.*

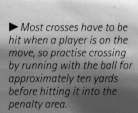

► *Most crosses have to be hit when a player is on the move, so practise crossing by running with the ball for approximately ten yards before hitting it into the penalty area.*

▲ *Ria Percival prepares to swing a cross into the penalty area during a 2015 Women's World Cup game between New Zealand and the Netherlands.*

Crossing the ball

A cross is simply a pass from out wide into the penalty area, but it can be deadly if hit with accuracy. Players work hard on their crossing and tend to use the instep-drive pass to hit the ball quickly into the target area. Aimless punts into the goal box are easily defended. Make sure you glance up to locate a target before you make a cross. You're looking to get the ball onto a teammate's head or in front of them for a snap shot. Hitting the byline means crossing from close to the end of the field. A cross from this position is harder for a goalie to defend because the ball tends to be moving away from him.

No.13 Gianfranco Zola

As well as having scored some classic goals, the skillful Italian forward also had the vision to pick out teammates in better positions than himself with unerring accuracy.

See also

12-13 Key Rules

30-31 Volleying and Shooting

42-43 Attacking Skills

Opening up Defenses

Many attacks break down as a result of slow or lazy thinking. Defensive techniques such as offside traps, where the entire defense move up in a line to catch forwards out, prey on sloppy attacking. Quick, accurate movement and passing can open up even the strongest of defenses.

Attacking passes and through balls

The closer you get to the opponent's goal, the less time and space there tends to be. A top-quality attacking pass should be placed and timed so that the receiver can do something with it when they first touch the ball. Passes for attackers to run on to must be carefully weighted so that they don't speed too far ahead of the receiver and get intercepted. Passes behind defenders, often known as "through balls," catch those defenders off guard but they require expert timing and teamwork between players.

▲ Christian Eriksen uses changes of speed, close control of the ball, and swerving the ball from side to side to beat defenders. The talented attacker has been Danish Player of the Year four times, in 2013, 2014, 2015, and 2018.

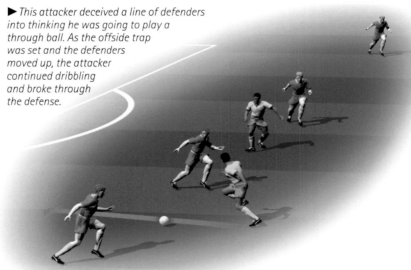

▶ This attacker deceived a line of defenders into thinking he was going to play a through ball. As the offside trap was set and the defenders moved up, the attacker continued dribbling and broke through the defense.

▲ The attacker on the left drags a defender out of position, just enough for a through ball to be played between the two defenders. The attacker on the right times his run to stay onside and collects the ball behind the defense.

Swerving passes

Swerving or bending the ball through the air is a technique often used when taking free kicks, but that is not its only value. During attacking moves the ability to swerve the ball can be very useful. Swerving the ball (see page 57) involves kicking through one side of it with a long follow through. This action puts sidespin on the ball which sends it off on a curved path. Inswinging and outswinging passes can clear opponents to find a teammate in a good position. Swerved shots can get around a defense and fool the opposition's goalie.

Scoring goals

A good attacking move doesn't guarantee a goal. For that you need a decisive finish from whoever receives the ball in a goalscoring position. The role of other attackers at this point is also crucial. In fact, following up a goalbound header or shot is vital because many goals at all levels come from rebounds off players or the goal. Good awareness is a vital quality in a forward as he or she must quickly judge which teammate is in the best position to attempt a goal.

No.14 Xavi Hernández

A winner of 28 major trophies with Barcelona and Spain, Xavi used his vision and excellent range of passes to open up even the tightest of defenses. He made over 180 assists for his Barcelona teammates throughout his career.

▲ *The on-ball player has a choice. He can cross the ball to the player on the right-hand side of the area using an outswinging swerved pass. Or he can simply send a short, straight pass to another free teammate.*

▲ *The player in yellow at the bottom of the picture gets into position, but at the last moment passes to a teammate at the top of the illustration who is in a much better position to tuck the ball away.*

MASTERCLASS
Opening up defenses

One-touch play, in which the ball is passed quickly between moving players, frequently creates openings.

Follow up any goal attempts by your team.

Don't be afraid to have a shot on goal if you are in the penalty area and no real alternative options are on offer.

▶ *Cristiano Ronaldo scores one of five goals during a 2015–2016 La Liga game against Espanyol. He also scored five for Real Madrid earlier in the year, against Granada. He remains the only player to score five goals in a match twice in Europe's top five leagues.*

Defending

See also

28-29 Tackling

48-49 Defending as a Unit

62-63 Formations

"Strikers win you games but defenders win you championships."

John Gregory

When the opposition has the ball, it's time to defend. Defending is sometimes seen as the least glamorous side of the game, but a goal prevented by a watchful, expert defense is just as valuable as a spectacular strike by your side. Skilled defenders are prized assets on all teams.

MASTERCLASS
Defending

As a team, you should close down space and reduce attacking options for the opposition.

Delay an opponent on the ball as much as you can by jockeying.

Never dribble out of your own penalty area when attackers lurk nearby. Look to pass the ball to teammates in plenty of space.

If in doubt, kick it out!

Regaining possession

Defending has two prime aims—to stop the opposition scoring and to regain possession of the ball. Regaining the ball can sometimes involve tackling, but there are other ways, such as jockeying and delaying an opponent, pressuring him into making a mistake. One vitally important method is closing down space. This involves you and your teammates getting into goalside positions, working together to cut out space for opposition attacks, and tracking attackers who run into dangerous positions.

▲ Cosmin Contra of Romania challenges Italy's Giorgio Chiellini for the ball. Tackling is just one way to regain possession of the ball.

Jockeying

Getting in the way of an attacker with the ball is a vital part of defending known as jockeying. When an opposition player with the ball approaches, close in on him. Don't close in too much—or he may find it easy to get around you—but enough to cut out open space in front of him. Get into a defensive stance with your body weight over your knees, standing on the balls of your feet, with your arms out for balance. Move with the player, keeping at a similar distance and staying goalside of him. By holding up the attacker, you are buying time for teammates to get back into stronger defensive positions.

◄ Calum Chambers jockeys Yannick Bolasie during an English Premier League game. Chambers closes in on his opponent, preventing him from turning easily.

Forcing a weaker position

Apart from delaying a player, jockeying is about forcing the attacker into a weaker position while staying goalside of him. One option is to try to guide him out toward a sideline—a less threatening position where he will have relatively little space and few options.

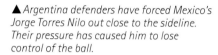

▲ *Argentina defenders have forced Mexico's Jorge Torres Nilo out close to the sideline. Their pressure has caused him to lose control of the ball.*

◄ *West Bromwich Albion's Saido Berahinio finds himself surrounded by Southampton defenders during a 2015 English Premier League game.*

From this position it may be easier to challenge him. If your opponent has his back to goal when receiving the ball, you are in a strong jockeying position and your main task is to prevent the player turning to face the goal without giving away a foul. Done well, jockeying may force a mistake, or at least a pass back and away from your goal. Stick with the attacker if he attempts to turn and run into space behind you.

▲ *Harriet Scott jockeys Ellen White in a women's match in England, preventing her from turning toward goal.*

◄ *South Korea's Kim Soo-yun (left) blocks a shot from Carli Lloyd using her foot during a 2015 international friendly in the United States.*

No.15 Bobby Moore

The captain of England's 1966 World Cup-winning side was a superb tackler and a great reader of the game. Pelé described him as, "the best defender I ever played against".

Get rid of it!

Great defenders such as Germany's Franz Beckenbauer were excellent at playing the ball skillfully out of defense before hitting an accurate pass to a teammate to set up an attacking move. However, even the very best defenders know that if the ball comes to them when under pressure, they should think safety first when making a clearance. This can mean safe passing into space, or when under severe pressure, getting plenty of height and distance on the ball to take it well away from the danger zone and your goal.

▲ *The defender in blue clears while under pressure from the attacker in yellow.*

See also

14-15 Fouls and Misconduct

28-29 Tackling

32-33 Heading

Defending as a Unit

Preventing an opposition attack leading to a goal is key to defending and the reason why teams defend as a unit. Attackers shouldn't expect the back four or five players and the goalkeeper do the work. Defending is the responsibility of all 11 players. There are different roles for different player positions, but many of the basic rules of defending apply to all.

▼ *Danish defender Lasse Nielsen clears the ball while under pressure from Ajax's Icelandic striker, Kolbeinn Sigthórsson.*

Defending from the front

Intelligent, committed defending begins at the front line and goes all the way back. The attackers' role in defense is an important one. They are the front line of defense, looking to restrict the opposition's space, chase down passes between opponents, and force these players to make mistakes. Good defensive work by attackers can put the opposition player on the ball under pressure. This can result in him making an aimless punt forward for your side to collect, or even an interception and immediate attacking chance.

Interception

Stealing the ball from the opposition as it travels from passer to receiver can be a clean, efficient way of regaining possession. It can also leave you with room to move away quickly and start an attack. Intercepting a ball simply requires speed and calls for quickness of thought, awareness of where players are, and judgment of the ball's speed and direction. In short you need to decide whether you can get to the ball before the opposition. A failed interception leaves the ball with your opponents and you out of position and out of the game.

MASTERCLASS
Defending as a unit

Don't dive in to intercept the ball or make a challenge until you have cover behind you.

Communication is vital when defending, especially at set pieces such as corners or free kicks.

Don't get distracted when marking—keep positioned to watch your opponent first and the game second.

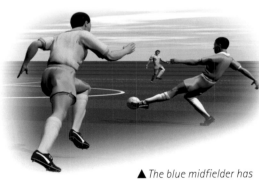

▲ *The blue midfielder has spotted an underhit pass and is about to make an interception. The farther from goal you are, the less risky this move becomes.*

◄ *A zonal defense system. When a forward enters a defender's zone (marked out by the dotted lines), defenders usually move in to mark that player. As an attacker moves out of one zone, the neighboring defender can pick him up.*

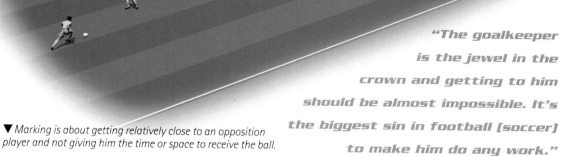

▶ A player-to-player marking system used in your side's defensive third of the field relies on additional players to act as spare defenders, putting the attacker on the ball under pressure.

No.16 Paolo Maldini

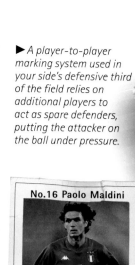

Able to spot danger from a distance, Maldini played as a sweeper, left-back, and in the center of defense for AC Milan and Italy. In 2007 he won his 5th Champions League medal.

▼ Marking is about getting relatively close to an opposition player and not giving him the time or space to receive the ball.

"The goalkeeper is the jewel in the crown and getting to him should be almost impossible. It's the biggest sin in football [soccer] to make him do any work."

George Graham

Defensive systems

There are two main ways in which a team works defensively as a unit. The first is by marking up player-to-player, where defenders mark one player and stick with him whenever the opposition is on the attack. The second system is zonal defense, where players are responsible for certain areas, or zones, of the field that all overlap, providing some cover. These zones can move up and down the field as the play dictates. Teams often mix systems, for example, playing a largely zonal defense, but giving one defender the task of player-marking a particularly dangerous attacker.

▼ Joel Lindpere of the New York Red Bulls stands by the near post ready to defend an opposition corner and make a goal line clearance if necessary.

▼ Marking up at set pieces, such as corners, is essential. The blue team have used their central defenders to mark the tallest attackers. Other players are positioned by the posts and the edge of the area.

See also

24-25 Movement and Space | 36-37 Fancy Skills | 48-49 Defending as a Unit

▲ *Mario Balotelli and Claudio Marchisio stand in the center circle as the kickoff begins to start their 2014 World Cup Group D match between Italy and England. The player who kicks off is not allowed to have the second touch of the ball.*

Restarts

Play can be stopped during a game for a number of reasons. These include when the ball leaves the field, a goal is scored, or a foul is committed. The way play is resumed depends on the kind of stoppage. For example, when the ball crosses a sideline, the officials will signal a throw-in. Corners, goal kicks, free kicks, kickoffs, and drop balls are other types of restarts.

The kickoff

Every game begins with a kickoff. This set piece is also played whenever a goal is scored and at the start of the second half. The ball has to be moved forward over the halfway line by the kicking-off team, while the opposition must stay in their half— but not enter the center circle—until the ball has been kicked. Many teams play the ball back after it has been tapped forward. Others launch a wide pass out to a flank, hoping that a winger can collect the ball and immediately attack the opposition's goalmouth.

◀ *Your hands should be spread around the back of the ball so that your thumbs almost touch. Too far around the sides and the ball can become harder to control.*

▶ *Placing your hands too close together around the back of the ball can lead you to lose grip as you make your throw.*

◀ *With feet firmly planted on the ground and ball behind your head, arch your back and thrust your upper body and arms forward. Release the ball just before your arms come over your head.*

▲ *This is a foul throw on three different reasons: the front foot is completely over the sideline, the trailing foot is off the ground, and only one hand is on the ball when the player makes the throw-in.*

Throw-ins

Throw-ins have to be taken from close to where the ball crossed the sideline. Officials usually penalize players who persistently try to gain extra ground before making the throw. Players of all standards are often penalized for foul throws. There are a few key rules you need to remember—your feet need to be behind the sideline, the ball brought back behind your head, and both hands have to be on the ball. Both feet have to be touching the ground as the throw is made and the ball is released. If you commit a foul throw, the opposing team is awarded the throw-in.

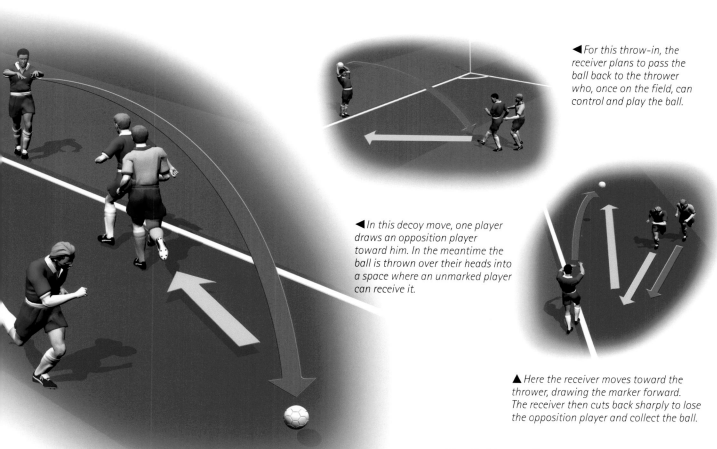

◄ For this throw-in, the receiver plans to pass the ball back to the thrower who, once on the field, can control and play the ball.

◄ In this decoy move, one player draws an opposition player toward him. In the meantime the ball is thrown over their heads into a space where an unmarked player can receive it.

▲ Here the receiver moves toward the thrower, drawing the marker forward. The receiver then cuts back sharply to lose the opposition player and collect the ball.

Longer throws

Long throws can get a ball directly into an opponent's penalty area. Even if you can't propel the ball that far, longer throws give you potentially more teammates to aim for and can be helpful for clearing the ball upfield. Take several quick steps up to the sideline and pull the ball right back behind your head. Arch your back as much as possible, then uncoil your back and arms to catapult the ball forward. Keep most of your weight on the front leg and follow through with your hands and fingers to direct the ball.

Don't throw it away

Treat throw-ins like you would any other set piece and practice a range of different throw-in moves. Avoid giving the ball away cheaply with a foul throw or a halfhearted throw that can be easily intercepted by the other side. Try to throw to a teammate who is unmarked and at a height that allows him to control the ball quickly and easily. Aim to throw to your teammate's feet, thigh, or head for a flick-on to another member of your team. A ball that bounces waist high in front of a player can be extremely difficult to control.

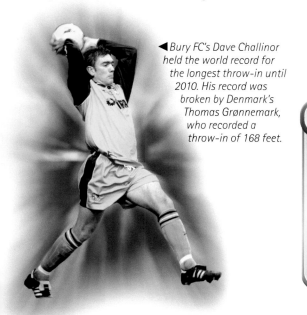

◄ Bury FC's Dave Challinor held the world record for the longest throw-in until 2010. His record was broken by Denmark's Thomas Grønnemark, who recorded a throw-in of 168 feet.

MASTERCLASS
Restarts

Plan and practice throw-in moves.

Try to lose your marker and get into a good position to receive a throw-in.

Stay alert to the possibilities of a quickly taken throw-in.

Practise different kinds of kickoffs.

▲ A drop ball is given when there has been a temporary break in play. Until the 2019-20 season, one player from each side would contest the ball (above). From 2019, the ball is dropped to a player on the team that last touched the ball. All other players must be at least 13 feet away.

See also

32-33 Heading

44-45 Opening up Defenses

48-49 Defending as a Unit

The Corner Kick

When a ball crosses a team's goal line and was last touched by a player from that team, the referee signals a corner kick. A corner is a dangerous situation for the defending team and a great opportunity for the attacking side.

Corner advantages

Corners are similar to crosses in open play, but with some big advantages—the ball isn't moving and you choose when to hit it. There are other pluses as well. Defenders have to be at least 10 yards away from the ball, you can have plenty of teammates in the penalty area as targets to aim for, and the offside rule doesn't apply. But there's also one disadvantage— defenders will be closely marking your team's players.

◀ *Teams practice different corner kicks in training. Here the player signals to his teammates what type of corner to expect.*

The art of a good corner kick

Good corners are hit with speed and accuracy—they should arrive in the target area a little above head height. Slow, high, looping corners are easily cleared by defenders. When you take a corner, you should feel completely balanced on your nonkicking foot and strike through the middle or just below the middle of the ball. The kicking leg follows through and across the body as the body turns into the cross.

No.17 Luis Figo

Portuguese striker Luis Figo was well known for the accuracy and power of his corner kicks. In 2000 he was bought by Spain's Real Madrid for what was then a record fee of over $65 million.

▲ *For a corner from the left-hand side of the pitch (from the attacking team's viewpoint), this is where you should place the ball if you're right-footed.*

Aiming long

Most corners are taken long and hit with enough power to reach the six-yard box or even closer to the goal. The classic target area is a point just in front of the near or far post. Inswinging corners swerve toward the goal, outswinging ones away from the goal. Both can be lethal.

◀ *This is where you should place the ball if you're left-footed. Using the left foot from this position can create an outswinging corner.*

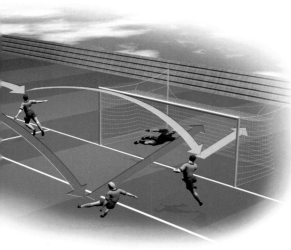

▶ *An inswinging corner usually bends into the six-yard box. Some inswinging corners have enough power and bend to hit the back of the net without being touched by another player.*

◀ *Near-post corners allow a flick-on header by a teammate (yellow arrows). Deeper corners toward the far post can give a teammate a chance to strike behind the goalie (red arrows).*

Speed and accuracy

Another advantage of a corner hit with speed is that it is harder for defenders to clear, and a mistake or deflection can easily lead to an own goal. When a corner is driven hard, teammates in the area may only need a touch rather than a power header or full-fledged shot to redirect the ball over the line.

▼ ▲ *During his time at Manchester United, David Beckham's corners led to many goals. Few were more important than Ole Gunnar Solskjaer's dramatic last-gasp winner in the 1999 Champions League final (above).*

MASTERCLASS
The corner kick

Aim for a target just above head height.

Strike the ball hard enough to carry it into the six-yard box.

Make sure you're completely balanced on your nonkicking foot.

Surprise your opponents with the occasional short corner.

Short corners

Taken quickly, short corners to a teammate a few feet away can allow the cross to come in from a different angle. They can catch the defending side off guard, with unmarked players in the box. But taken sloppily or slowly, they just waste a golden opportunity, leaving you or your teammate stranded in the corner.

See also

22–23 Advanced Passing

24–25 Movement and Space

56–57 Free Kicks in Attack

Free Kicks

If a team commits an offence, they can expect the referee to blow his whistle and award a free kick to the other side. A free kick sees the ball placed on the ground at the point where the offence was committed, while the opposing team is forced to retreat at least ten yards (9.15 meters). Not every free kick offers an attacking chance but all give a side valuable possession in time and in space.

▲ One exception to the ten-yard rule occurs when a team is awarded an indirect free kick inside the opponent's penalty area. The defenders are allowed to stand on their goal line even if it isn't ten yards away from the free kick.

▲ Referee Nicola Rizzoli uses vanishing spray foam to mark the place where Argentina's Lionel Messi is to take a free kick. The spray is used to show the ten yards between ball and defenders at free kicks clearly. It was first used in an international competition in 2011— the Copa Libertadores.

▼ Referee Lee Mason signals that an indirect free kick has been awarded. His arm will remain in the air until the kick is taken and has either touched another player or gone out of play.

▼ Colombian midfielder Yoreli Rincón whips a free kick into the Mexican penalty area during the 2015 FIFA Women's World Cup.

Turn defense into attack

Wherever you are on the field, a free kick gives you the great gift of possession—so don't waste it. Quick free kicks can open up attacking opportunities, but only if you and the receiver are alert, the free kick is hit accurately, and no opponent can intercept it. When awarded a free kick deep in your own half, aim to get the ball out of your danger zone and move possession farther upfield. Don't put your side in danger by hitting a lazy ball or playing the ball to a teammate who's not expecting the pass. Be aware and look around for a free player.

Indirect free kicks

An indirect free kick is so called because you cannot score directly from it—instead the ball must be played by one other teammate before a goal attempt can be made. Indirect free kicks are given for less serious offenses in soccer, including charging or obstructing a player who isn't on the ball or receiving the ball in an offside position. Goalkeepers can incur indirect free kicks if, for example, they hold onto the ball for more than the allowed six seconds or handle a deliberate back pass.

▲ *Bastian Oczipka, playing for Eintracht Frankfurt, attempts to bend the ball round VfB Stuttgart's defensive wall to target the goal.*

MASTERCLASS
Free kicks

Rehearse your free kicks as a team hard and often. Split up into defenders and attackers to create as realistic a situation as possible.

Keep your free-kick moves simple and effective. A move that requires more than three touches exposes it to more possibilities to break down.

Vary free kicks during a game to keep opponents guessing.

▲ *The arrows show some of the options possible from this direct free kick—bending the ball around one side of the wall of defenders, a shot up and over the wall, or rolling the ball out to the side for a teammate to strike.*

Direct free kicks

For the more serious offences, including pushing and tripping, or a goalkeeper handling outside of his area, teams get a direct free kick. This is where the first touch can, but doesn't have to be, a direct shot on goal. Direct free kicks in central positions in the attacking-third of the field can offer many options and are a real menace to defend against, even with a wall in place. Players and teams practise their free-kick moves long and hard to try to turn the threat into goalscoring reality.

▶ *Gareth Bale strikes an expert free kick with the inside of his foot. His weight is balanced over the ball as he strikes it to keep it down and on target.*

See also

30–31 Volleying and Shooting

52–53 The Corner Kick

54–55 Free Kicks

Free Kicks in Attack

Free kicks give you one touch of the ball without being challenged and with the opposition some distance away. In an attacking position this is a priceless commodity. Many games are decided on the results of free kicks, so the attacking side needs to take advantage of it, and defenders must be alert and vigilant.

▲ Crystal Palace players form a wall to defend a free kick. Communication between the outfield players and goalie is essential to position the wall in the right place.

▲ For long-range or wide free kicks, a two- or three-man wall is frequently used. When the free kick is central and close to goal, teams build a five- or six-man wall.

Defending a free kick

As soon as the ref gives a free kick to the opposition, get back into a defensive position. Stay alert for a quickly taken free kick—if it doesn't come, get organized, and listen to teammates' instructions. It's vital to get players behind the ball, covering the spaces where a goalscoring chance might be created. If the free kick is likely to be a cross, taller defenders should mark good headers of the ball, while other defenders look to cut out knock-downs and pick up attackers making late runs into the box.

▲ A sidefoot pass can change the angle of attack and give the receiver the chance of a shot without the defensive wall blocking his way.

Surprise and disguise

Some element of surprise is often required for free kicks to be successful. Don't let it be obvious what you plan to do to the opposing side—it will make the free kick easy to defend. Decoy runs by players can cause confusion and mask the planned free-kick attempt. Attackers can form a wall in front of the real wall to hide the ball. Until 2019–20, attackers could join the end of a defensive wall (pictured above), aiming to block the goalie's view or create a gap for the shot to travel through. From 2019, attackers can only stand next to a one- or two-player wall.

Bending the ball

A useful skill to have on the pitch during open play, the ability to bend or swerve the ball accurately can be deadly at free kicks. Expert free-kick takers such as Neymar, Lionel Messi, Cristiano Ronaldo, and Antoine Griezmann all have this skill. It's a complicated technique that requires much practice and perseverance, and some players find they're better at hitting inside swerves or outside swerves. Both types of swerve involve hitting the ball low through one side and finishing with a long, relaxed follow-through.

▲ *To hit an inside swerve (left), strike the ball with the inside of your cleat, using a straight follow-through. For an outside swerve (right), use the outside of your cleat—the follow-through should take your foot across your body.*

Fast or wide

The quickly taken free kick isn't only used in the middle of the field to put the ball into space. A rapid move, such as a snap shot from a direct free kick, can catch a goalkeeper and his defense off guard—just ask the French team Lille, who lost a 2007 Champions League game against England's Manchester United to a quick free kick by Ryan Giggs. Wide free kicks can also offer more options than just a simple, immediate cross. An overlap down the wing can send in a cross from a more threatening angle, and a ball infield to a late-arriving runner can offer a shooting chance.

▼ *The options from this position include bending the ball in for a cross, passing the ball infield, or playing it down the wing for a wide player to cross from the goal line.*

▶ *Players on the attacking side peel off from the defensive wall, causing confusion among their opponents as the free-kick taker attempts a shot on goal.*

MASTERCLASS
Free kicks in attack

Listen to your goalie and other players when forming the defensive wall.

When defending, stay alert to the possibility of a sudden, surprise free kick.

Work hard on learning to bend the ball. It will assist your free kick and corner taking, as well as your long passing and shooting in open play.

▲ *All successful sides, from local or school teams right up to Brazil's national team (pictured), work on their free kick moves during training.*

No.18 Roberto Carlos

Brazilian World Cup winner Roberto Carlos is perhaps best known for scoring a stunning, swerving, and dipping free kick from more than 82 ft. out, against France in 1997.

See also

12–13 Key Rules

14–15 Fouls and Misconduct

30–31 Volleying and Shooting

Penalty!

A penalty kick is a free shot on goal taken from the penalty spot. Any foul where a direct free kick would normally be awarded becomes a penalty if the foul was committed inside the box. To give a penalty, referees have to judge where the foul was committed—not where the fouled player ended up. For the attacking side, a penalty is a goal in the making.

▲ When a penalty is given, only the referee, goalkeeper, and penalty taker are allowed in the penalty area until the penalty taker has made contact with the ball. A referee can order a penalty to be retaken if any other players from either team enter the area.

▲ The penalty taker starts his run up, noting the goalie's position. Most penalty takers have decided what sort of penalty they intend before they move toward the ball.

▲ This player has approached the ball as if he is going to put it toward the right side of the goal as he views it. The goalie starts to move in that direction as the kick is taken.

▲ The penalty taker wraps his foot around the ball and uses a firm, low sidefoot pass to place the ball into the opposite corner of the goal.

The mental game

Ronaldo, Gerrard, Messi—these and many more star players have all missed penalty kicks in crucial situations. So how do top players miss such clear chances on goal? In a single word—pressure. In a few more words—pressure and plenty of time for a player's thoughts to get the better of him. The good news is that at all levels of soccer if you can stay relaxed and focused, the task in front of you is relatively simple. You're just 11 yards away from goal, with only the goalie to beat. The odds are certainly stacked in the penalty taker's favor.

Chip, blast, or place

For professional players, the choice of penalty shot to use is great. Some players prefer the simple chip over a diving goalie into the back of the middle of the net. Many choose to blast the ball as hard as possible or aim a driven shot into a corner. Add the possibility of feints and fakes during the run up, and the pregame preparation, which involves studying rivals' penalty takers and goalkeepers, and it soon becomes a confusing array of options. The placed penalty is the most popular choice for amateur players. This is a relatively simple shot made with the side of the foot, hitting the ball firmly but under control into one of the goal's four corners.

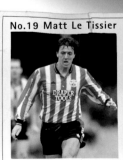

No.19 Matt Le Tissier

Matt Le Tissier retired in 2002, but he will always be a legend at English Premier League team Southampton, in part due to his success with penalty kicks. In his time with the team, he scored 48 penalties from 49 attempts.

▲ *Dutch goalkeeper Tim Krul makes a stunning one-handed penalty save from Costa Rica's Michael Umaña during the 2014 FIFA World Cup. Krul was brought on as a substitute goalie especially for the penalty shootout by manager Louis van Gaal and made two saves as the Dutch won 4-3*

The goalie's view

As a goalie facing a penalty, you should be calm and relaxed. A goal from a penalty is expected, but if the opposition push or blast the kick high or wide, you'll be delighted; but if you actually save their attempt, you're the top dog. From the 2019–20 season, keepers must not be moving or touching the goalposts when the kick is taken, and they must have part of one foot on or in line with the goal line. Some goalies, just like penalty takers, decide in advance which way to go and dive at full-stretch as the kick is taken, or choose instead to remain standing. Others try to read the taker's intentions, or if they've come up against the taker before, try to recall the most likely direction.

▼ *Practice penalties using a goal and two cones, each placed 3 feet in from the goalposts. Aim to send your kicks between the cones and the goalposts.*

MASTERCLASS
Penalty!

Decide early where you intend to put the penalty, and don't change your mind in the run up.

Keep your head down and your body balanced as you take the kick.

Stay alert and aware after taking a regular penalty for a second chance following a save. Other players should follow up after the kick has been taken to both attack and defend.

▲ *U.S. national team goalkeeper Alyssa Naeher saves a penalty during the 2019 Women's World Cup semifinal against England. The 84th-minute save was crucial in securing the U.S. a 2–1 win and a place in the final.*

▲ *Italian Roberto Baggio is upset after blazing his 1994 World Cup final penalty over the crossbar, handing the trophy to Brazil.*

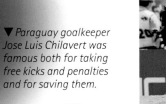

▼ *Paraguay goalkeeper Jose Luis Chilavert was famous both for taking free kicks and penalties and for saving them.*

Penalty shootouts

Many knockout competitions use penalty shootouts to decide the outcome of a game when the scores are still even after overtime. A shootout usually calls for five players on each side to take alternate penalties, and if the score is even after those ten kicks, more players, one from each side, continue until there is a winner. Although labelled as cruel on individuals, penalty shootouts are pure theater, and many believe a fairer way of deciding the outcome than drawing straws or flipping a coin.

▲ *Italy's Fabio Grosso scores the winning penalty in the 2006 World Cup final, which went to a penalty shootout. Italy made up for its defeat in the 1994 final with a 5-3 shootout victory over France.*

▲ Despite guiding Real Madrid to the Spanish league title in 2003, Vicente del Bosque was fired. He bounced back to coach Spain, who became World Cup winners (2010) and European champions twice (2008, 2012).

"You must believe you are the best and then make sure that you are."

Bill Shankly

Managers and Coaches

No one feels the pressures of soccer more than the person in charge of shaping the team, selecting the players who will play and in what positions, and choosing the tactics. At some teams this responsibility is split between a director of soccer, who oversees the team's development and is involved with transfers, and a first-team manager or coach, who works with the players. At other teams, it's all down to one individual, usually known as the manager.

▼ A passion for the game and the ability to motivate players are hallmarks of successful managers such as Liverpool legend Bill Shankly, who transformed his team.

◀ Many ex-pros move into management. Others work behind the scenes, coaching players. Here, Gary Neville coaches his former Manchester United teammates Wayne Rooney and Michael Carrick, as well as James Milner, when he was England's first-team coach.

Head of a team

Although they usually receive most of the attention, modern-day managers and coaches tend to be part of a large team of backroom staff. They frequently employ a second-in-command, an assistant coach who helps with the day-to-day running of the first-team squad. There are often additional coaches in charge of the youth and reserve teams as well as scouts who scour regions, countries, and even continents on the lookout for fresh talent. Fitness trainers, physical therapists and other medical staff, uniform assistants, and sometimes sports psychologists who help to focus the players mentally, complete what is a good-sized team, all working behind the scenes for a team.

▲ Former England manager Steve McClaren (right) urges his Newcastle United team on during a 2015–2016 English Premier League match versus Southampton. Sammy Lee, Southampton's assistant coach, is also on the sidelines.

Pressure cooker

Despite being part of a team, the manager or coach of a club can often find himself under immense pressure, especially at top teams for which success is expected. Managers' reputations stand or fall on their player selections, their transfer dealings, and by the tactical decisions they make in individual games or over a season. But above all, managers are judged on their results. It can take only a handful of disappointing scorelines for managers to be criticized in the media and by fans and owners. Continued failings inevitably lead to speculation over their future employment. In the past, many managers spent decades at the same team. Today, with the financial stakes much higher and the pressure to deliver trophies much greater, many teams change managers frequently. For example, about half of the 20 English Premier League clubs have bosses that have been in their current positions for less than a year.

▲ Sometimes managers outlast their chairmen. Here, Arsenal's Arsène Wenger discusses matters with chairman David Dein in 2001. Dein left the team in 2007 while Wenger did not leave until more than a decade later, in 2018.

▲ Real Madrid welcome Zinedine Zidane in 2001 after he was signed for more than $75 million, a world record fee at the time.

▲ Some of Europe's top managers and head coaches including Arsène Wenger (bottom left), Josep Guardiola (bottom right) and Frank de Boer (middle row, right) pose for a photo at a UEFA coaching meeting.

◀ Argentina's César Luis Menotti controversially left Diego Maradona off his 1978 World Cup team, but won the tournament.

A manager's duties

An excellent soccer brain, top-notch people and decision-making skills, and a vision of how the team will develop and should play are vital requirements for the modern manager or coach. A manager's tasks include structuring the players' coaching and practicing, dealing with the media, working on specific skills, playing styles, and set pieces, and checking out upcoming opponents and possible transfer targets. In addition a manager has to assess the form and ability of new players, youngsters, and players returning from injury, deciding when to play them and in what position.

▶ Liverpool manager Jürgen Klopp celebrates winning the 2019 Champions League final against Tottenham.

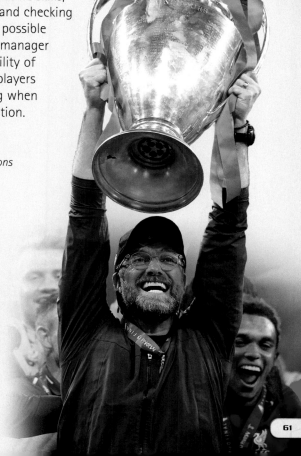

Team and country

With soccer teams a big business, particularly in Europe, a manager's ability to wheel and deal profitably in the transfer market is considered a major asset. Some managers have earned themselves excellent reputations for their uncanny knack of buying players cheaply and selling them on at a later date for a much higher fee. An astute transfer swoop can invigorate and inspire a team and bring them honor. Replacing valued players with underperforming ones, on the other hand, often leads to being fired. National managers don't have the pressure of dealing with transfers, but instead they must endure the major headache of selecting a successful team from a much wider base of players. They must also be able to cope with the phenomenal pressure and the expectations of an entire nation. Be it team or country, all managers fear failure and dream of the glory and satisfaction that comes with success.

Formations

All soccer teams need a structure with players organized into a basic shape called a formation. Formations tend to be described in terms of the numbers of outfield players, from the defense forward. So 4-4-2 describes a system of four defenders, four midfielders, and finally two attackers. The following are some of the most important formations and systems in soccer history.

"Football [soccer] is self-expression within an organized framework."

Roger Lemerre, former French national coach

Major William Sudell
of Preston North End
(England)

2-3-5

Preston North End coach Major William Sudell was just one of many managers to adopt the first commonly used formation, 2-3-5. It featured five forwards with three midfielders, known as halfbacks, and just one pair of fullbacks defending the goal. The key player was the center-half, who played in the middle of the field and was the main playmaker in attack, but also had to get back to mark the opposition team's center-forward. While sides in Europe and South America toyed with a variety of different formations, most teams in the U.K. stuck with 2-3-5 until the mid-1920s.

W-M (3-2-2-3)

Changes to the offside law for the 1925-1926 season initially saw teams struggle to contain a five-man attack. After a 7-0 defeat to another English team, Newcastle United, Arsenal manager Herbert Chapman decided to pull his center-half back into defense and move two of his forwards back into midfield. Arsenal beat West Ham (England) 4-0 with this new W-M formation two days later. It was called "W-M" because the forwards formed a "W" shape, and the defenders an "M" shape. Many other sides adopted this system, and for a quarter of a century it was used all over the world.

Arsenal manager
Herbert Chapman
(England)

4-2-4

Brazil, under the management of Vicente Feola, arrived at the 1958 World Cup finals with two secret weapons: a 17-year-old attacker we now know as Pelé and a system designed to counter the old W-M formation. The 4-2-4 system saw a strong defensive line of four players, with two midfielders controlling and directing play for a pair of wingers and two central strikers. Although this formation proved successful for Brazil and some other teams, it is rarely used in the modern game as it places too much emphasis on the midfield players, who may be outnumbered.

Vicente Feola (Brazil)

Catenaccio (1-4-3-2)

Italian for "big chain," *catenaccio* means creating a defensively strong side, often at the expense of the attack. Central to this formation is the role of the sweeper, who plays behind the defense, mopping up loose balls and covering challenges. Under Helenio Herrera, coach of the highly successful Inter Milan team of the 1960s, *catenaccio* frequently stifled opposition attacks. Teams playing this system often relied on fast breaks by small numbers of attackers to score.

Helenio Herrera, coach
of Inter Milan (Italy)

4-3-3

From the 1960s onward soccer tactics became increasingly defensive. Even the most attack-minded of international sides, such as Brazil, withdrew one of their forwards back into midfield to play with a 4-3-3 formation. Brazil won the World Cup in 1962 and 1970 with this system. 4-3-3 is still used to this day, but mostly by attack-minded teams intent on stretching their opponents. Exciting Spanish team Barcelona won the 2009 UEFA Champions League using a 4-3-3 formation, featuring playsers like Thierry Henry, the talented Argentinian Lionel Messi, and Samuel Eto'o.

Aymoré Moreira led
Brazil to glory in 1962

4-4-2

4-4-2 is one of the most commonly used formations in modern soccer. One of the first to use it was England manager Sir Alf Ramsey, whose "wingless wonders" won the 1966 World Cup. It provides two waves of four players to close down and defend, but the two strikers need to cover a lot of ground and must receive support in attacks. Variations include 4-1-3-2, where one midfielder sits in front of the defense and breaks up attacks, and 4-4-1-1, where one striker plays behind his partner. Italy won the 2006 World Cup playing 4-4-1-1.

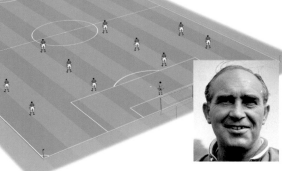

England manager
Sir Alf Ramsey

3-2-3-2

Inspired by Dutch coach Rinus Michels, "total football [soccer]" saw a team's players interchange positions and roles fluidly, a system that required every player to be comfortable on the ball. It is rare to see "total football" today. More common are 4-4-2 and the 3-2-3-2, or wing-back, formations. The two key features of this latter formation are the three center-backs, one of whom may be asked to man-on-man mark an opposing striker and the two wide players—the wing-backs. Wing-backs have to cover the entire length of a field, linking up in midfield and attack, as well as defending.

Rinus Michels (Holland)

Tactics

Within the chosen basic formation, a manager or coach has plenty of room to try out different tactics, systems, and ploys. Over the last 50 years there have been a great number of innovations in tactical thinking that have seen subtle alterations to certain formations. There has also been a development of moves and tactics within these formations.

▶ *Sweepers such as Italy's Gaetano Scirea can play defensively—rarely straying ahead of fellow defenders—or can move up to attack.*

▲ *Brazil star Dani Alves is one of the world's best modern wing-backs. He's able to play fullback in defense but can sprint up the wing to start and join attacks.*

Options and systems

There are many variations and options within each formation. For example, sweepers can be used defensively or as a potential attacking weapon (see illustration top left).

The same is the case for a system featuring wing-backs (left). Wing-backs can be instructed to stay back, creating a five-man defense. Alternatively they can move back and forth, helping out in defense and attack, or they can surge forward, becoming wingers and creating an overload up front.

Another option in midfield and attack is called the diamond system. This involves four midfielders, or three midfielders and a striker, forming a diamond shape on the field. At the head of the diamond, farthest upfield, is an attacking midfielder or striker who makes late runs into position and links the midfield with the attack. Because the diamond system creates a great deal of depth up front, it can be hard for teams to defend.

◀ *The diamond formation offers plenty of options for the team going forward.*

In the hole

Many sides play a pair of attackers or just a lone striker in the most forward position with another player positioned behind the front line. This player plays in what is called "the hole" and can be a massive threat to the opposition. He stays onside and can prompt attacks by precise passing and through balls, or if defenders back off, he can advance and unleash a long-range shot.

◀ *Daniele De Rossi battles hard for the ball with Germany's Mesut Özil during their Euro 2012 semifinal match. De Rossi usually plays as a midfield "anchor" playing in front of the defense and breaking up attackers.*

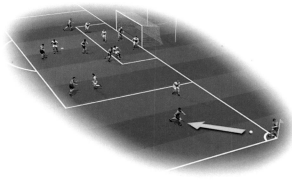

▲ *There is always a risk involved in playing the offside trap, and that applies even when an attack develops from a short corner, as is the case in the above illustration.*

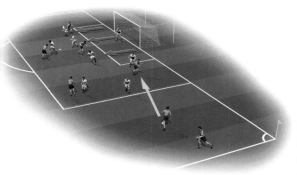

▲ *The attacker shapes to pass to a teammate (yellow arrow). Most of the defense has moved upfield but the defender marking the likely receiver keeps him onside.*

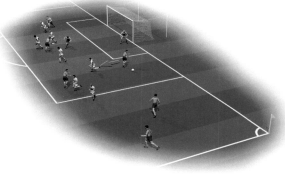

▲ *The defender must step up before the ball is played to force the attacker offside. If the defender is not quick enough, the attacker would have a good chance to score.*

▼ *Mali's Falaye Sacko uses a long throw to get the ball close to Serbia's goal quickly during a FIFA U20 World Cup match in 2015.*

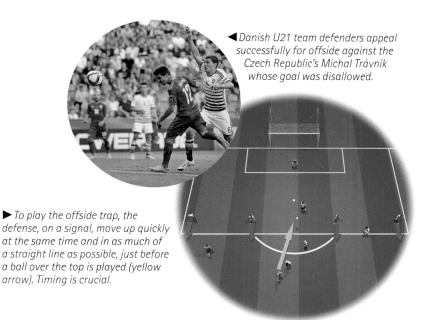

◄ *Danish U21 team defenders appeal successfully for offside against the Czech Republic's Michal Trávník whose goal was disallowed.*

▶ *To play the offside trap, the defense, on a signal, move up quickly at the same time and in as much of a straight line as possible, just before a ball over the top is played (yellow arrow). Timing is crucial.*

The offside trap

When an attacker is offside, possession passes to the defending team so many sides adopt a defensive tactic known as the offside trap to make this happen as often as possible. The offside trap involves the back three or four players maintaining a straight line across the field as they suddenly move upfield to catch an opponent offside. Performed well, the offside trap can be infuriating for the opposition, but it does carry the risk of being sprung, leaving no defensive cover during an attack.

▶ *Players may aim for a tall, physical striker such as Belgium's Romelu Lukaku with long passes upfield.*

The long-ball game

Some teams prefer to build attacks patiently with the emphasis on keeping possession and switching the direction of play to probe an opposition defense for an opening. A contrasting tactic is rapid and direct. A long-ball pass out of defense or midfield to an advanced attacker can quickly open up a game. The role of this target player is to get to the ball first and then control it. From there, he may either turn and attack the goal himself or hold onto the ball long enough to open up a teammate who has arrived in support. For a defender it is possible to largely bypass the midfield and send long balls up to the strikers.

Tactics in a Game

▲ *A fourth official holds up his electronic board to indicate a substitution.*

Once the game starts managers have to hope that their formation, tactics, and player selection all conspire to give their team victory. But it doesn't always work out that way. Opposition teams can spring tactical surprises, and decisions and luck can go against a team, and certain players can be lacking certain skills. In order to react to such events, managers can make extra changes to their team's tactics and play throughout the entire game.

Assessing the game

From kickoff onward managers and their coaching staff study the action, checking out the opposition's tactics and looking for weaknesses or mismatches on either side. For the players involved in the game, it can be hard to assess how things are going beyond the scoreline. Managers are far better positioned to judge both the game and how individuals are faring. Is a player slightly injured and not performing to his best? Is a defender getting pulled out of position by one particularly tricky attacker? Is the opposition's offside trap weak and liable to be sprung? These and a dozen other questions will be occupying the manager or coach's thoughts.

▲ *Cesc Fàbregas (left) is replaced by Oscar during Chelsea's 2014-2015 Champions League game against Paris Saint-Germain. Top players have to accept a place on the bench at times.*

◀ *During the 1999 Champions League final, Sir Alex Ferguson (left) instructs substitute Teddy Sheringham (right), who went on to score Manchester United's goal to tie in injury time.*

MASTERCLASS
A winning attitude

Prepare for every game as if it were the biggest of the season.

As a substitute warm up well before coming on. This will help you get up to speed in a game.

Don't ease up when your team is ahead. Too many games swing back the other way.

Accept the manager's decision to substitute you or play you in a different position.

Substitutions

Substitutions are a vital part of a manager's armory. He can replace a player who is injured, not performing, or just needs a rest. A manager can also sacrifice a player in order to bring on another type of player. Two common substitutions are to bring off a striker when your team is winning by several goals or to replace a defender with an extra attacker when your side is behind.

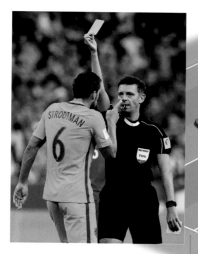

▲ Dutch midfielder Kevin Strootman is sent off in a 2018 World Cup qualifying defeat against France.

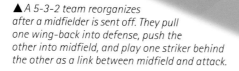

▲ A 5-3-2 team reorganizes after a midfielder is sent off. They pull one wing-back into defense, push the other into midfield, and play one striker behind the other as a link between midfield and attack.

▲ Communication is vital in marshaling a team, as Swiss goalie Yann Sommer demonstrates.

Changing tactics

Some coaches toy constantly with tactics during a game; other coaches prefer to leave things pretty much as they are. But they all want their sides to get and maintain possession, to look secure in defense, and to be effective in attack. As a game develops managers spot weaknesses in both teams and look to fix their own while exploiting those of the opposition. For example, a manager may pull a midfielder back to track and guard a dangerous opposition attacker who plays deep.

▶ Encouraging teammates, as U.S. goalkeeper Hope Solo (top right) is doing, helps maintain confidence. The Korea Republic team (right) build morale as they huddle just before kickoff. Listening to the advice and support of teammates is important for strong team spirit.

A winning attitude

The best coaches in the world won't succeed unless their players have the right attitude. Coaches and managers seek to instill a winning attitude in their teams so that even when things are going against them, the players continue to work hard to turn things around. But what is a winning attitude in practical terms? It involves keeping your confidence when your team is being overrun. It means not picking on your own teammates when they make a mistake, but encouraging them. Above all, it means concentrating and working not as individuals, but as a team.

"You can play any style that you like, the important thing is to create a strong group."
Cesare Maldini

A Pro's Life

Throughout the world millions of children, teenagers, and amateur adult players turn out for their local teams every week. Of these, it's a fairly safe bet that most, if not all, of them dream of one day getting paid to play soccer and eventually, reaching the very top of the professional game.

▲ *Thousands of amateur games, like this weekend game played on the outskirts of London, England, feature players who dream of a chance to be paid to play professional soccer for a top team.*

A long, long road

Gifted youngsters may be the best midfielders or strikers in their school, area, or even region, but they face a long, uphill path before they can join the top ranks. Many never make the grade and others falter after joining a soccer club as a youth player, never completing the step up to the reserves and the first team. Disappointment is rife, but some players are lucky enough to be given a second chance.

▶ *Coach Wim Jonk (left) and Dutch legend Johan Cruyff watch young players train at Ajax Academy. Ajax is famous for producing many star players including Frenkie de Jong, Toby Alderweireld, and Cruyff himself.*

▲ *A team with a rich crop of youngsters has a greater chance of a rosy future. Manchester United's (England) youth team of the early 1990s, pictured here after their 1992 FA Youth Cup win, contained players such as Ryan Giggs, David Beckham, Gary Neville, and Nicky Butt—who became star players.*

Pro health

Top players are expensive assets and teams strive to keep them as healthy and fit as possible. The days of eating greasy food prior to a game are long gone. Diet and bodyweight are monitored carefully, and foods packed with carbohydrates such as vegetables, pastas, and rice are typical fare. Minor injuries or tiredness often result in a player losing form and possibly his place in the team. The biggest fear of most professionals is a major injury, that can keep them out for many months, or even end their career.

▶ *Players receive immediate attention when they get injured during a game. Here Manchester United defender Luke Shaw is treated for a head injury during a 2015 English Premier League game.*

▲ *Injured professionals may spend many hours working with physical therapists to recover.*

▲ Midfieder Luis Figo attends a glamorous function with his wife, Helene. Particularly in Europe, top stars are major celebrities, often seen at gallery openings, movie premieres, and exclusive parties.

▲ George Best, England's original soccer superstar, was one of the first to employ a business manager (second left), pictured next to Best along with Best's secretary (left) and chauffeur (right).

Playing for a living

The majority of professional soccer players earn a fraction as much as Cristiano Ronaldo and Lionel Messi. With relatively short playing careers and the threat of injury always present, more and more players use agents to negotiate good contracts and transfer deals on their behalf. Agents and certain freedom of work laws and court rulings have helped engineer far more player movement between European teams than ever before.

Rewards and responsibilities

The rewards for making it to the top are huge. Massive salaries, measured in tens of thousands of dollars per week, are just the start. Sponsorships and endorsements of a company's products can quickly make star players multimillionaires, and that's before money from personal appearances, media work, and cuts from a transfer deal. All this comes at a price, however. The pressure to perform and media intrusion are two of the negative aspects of a pro's life.

▲ The money is great, but most players dream of the glory of lifting a trophy more than anything else. Here, U.S. star Megan Rapinoe celebrates with the FIFA Women's World Cup trophy in 2019, alongside midfielder Allie Long.

▲ The Ballon d'Or is an annual award for the world's best player. Cristiano Ronaldo (above) and Lionel Messi have each won it a record five times.

▶ England defender Laura Bassett signs autographs for eager fans in Canada at the 2015 Women's World Cup.

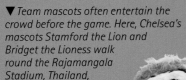

▼ *Team mascots often entertain the crowd before the game. Here, Chelsea's mascots Stamford the Lion and Bridget the Lioness walk round the Rajamangala Stadium, Thailand, in 2015.*

Teams and fans

Especially in Europe and South America, the bond between fans and their team is powerful. Fans may chant for a manager to leave, or be unhappy with certain players or the current team, but their love of the team itself remains. Many fans travel the world to show their support for their team.

An emotional rollercoaster

Whether it's your national team, your favorite professional team or a local amateur team you support, soccer games generate a range of intense feelings. From the dreadful low of seeing your team knocked out of an important competition to the incredible high of watching a spectacular winning goal by your team, the emotional rollercoaster ride you can experience is addictive—which is why most fans support the same team for their entire life.

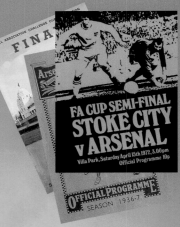

▲ *The game day program is essential pregame and halftime reading for many fans.*

▶ *A stall sells replica shirts, scarves, and other merchandise to fans before a Champions League game between Bayern Munich and AS Roma.*

▼ *Paris St. Germain fans proclaim their support for their team with a sea of banners and flares during a Champions League encounter with English team Chelsea.*

All dressed up

To be a lifelong fan of a soccer team is like being part of a close-knit tribe. In Europe and South America, fans learn their own team's chants and songs, wear the team colors, and buy many team-related products known as merchandise. Merchandising has become an important money-maker for professional teams with sales of shirts and other items often exceeding the money made by ticket sales.

The big game

Many fans get excited long before the start of a new season or before an important game. Derby games, where a team plays their local rivals, tend to produce the most intense atmospheres. Derbies between Spanish rivals Real Madrid and Barcelona, Italian giants Internazionale and AC Milan, and the Scottish "Old Firm" games between Celtic and Rangers are among the biggest clashes.

◀▼ Fans can generate an incredible atmosphere, few more so than the supporters of the Reggae Boyz (left)—the nickname of Jamaica's national team. International games are an occasion to celebrate your country, as these face-painted U.S. soccer fans demonstrate.

▲ *Floral tributes left at Anfield stadium in England, home of Liverpool FC. The tributes were in response to the 1989 Hillsborough tragedy in which 96 Liverpool fans died.*

▲ *A stall outside Atlético Madrid stadium sells scarves, flags, and other merchandise to fans before Atlético's Europa League game versus Hannover 96.*

Trouble and tragedy

Throughout soccer's history there have been incidents of violence, accidents, and tragedy. The intense passion of some fans can overstep the mark, turning to hatred, abuse, and violence toward players, officials and, in particular, fans of rival teams. Outbreaks of hooliganism and crowd trouble have blighted the game in Europe and South America, but more intelligent policing and the use of video cameras has led to many arrests. After a number of tragedies—including people being crushed as crowds of standing fans surged forward, or were unable to escape from fire—many stadiums have become less-crowded, all-seater venues with more attention paid to safety.

Soccer Media

Playing soccer and watching it live in a stadium are only two of the ways in which fans can immerse themselves in the game. Reading about soccer in newspapers and magazines, surfing the Internet, picking up scores from the radio, or watching highlights on television all allow people to follow the sport they love.

The press
Newspapers in South America and Europe have back pages devoted to sports news, interviews, results, rumors, and gossip with soccer tending to dominate on a day-to-day basis.

◀ Fans have a variety of options to choose from when it comes to finding out more about the game, such as magazines, newspapers, and sports shows on TV.

▲ Websites, including this official site for Italian side Roma, allow fans to keep up to date with their team.

▼ The first television filming of soccer came in 1936 when the British Broadcasting Corporation (BBC) filmed a demonstration game featuring Arsenal and Everton players.

Some publications are often criticized for being too harsh on players, unsettling them with rumors of transfers, and seeking to inflame disagreements and generate scandals. However, there's no doubt that the press stirs up enthusiasm and interest in the sport, allowing fans to obtain game reports and features on famous players and managers. Some fans of teams, players, or a particular competition produce publications for other fans. Known as fanzines, these publications are independent of teams and offer ordinary fans the chance to put their often critical opinions in print, thus reaching a wider audience.

▼ Television coverage has advanced greatly since the early days with enhanced statistics and here, a map showing where on the field Eden Hazard controlled or passed the ball during a game for Chelsea.

Eden Hazard v Swansea
Touch map
Source: OPTA

◀ Cameramen on mobile platforms provide exciting views of the game at field level for TV audiences.

◀ *Almost every angle is covered by TV cameras, including the bird's-eye view offered by this Goodyear blimp.*

Television coverage

Television, more than any other media outlet, has been responsible for the explosion of interest in soccer. The broadcasting of soccer today is a sophisticated operation involving many different camera angles, a soundtrack provided by commentators and pundits, and a whole host of behind-the-scenes technical staff.

New views and choices

Soccer has pushed television technology to provide new and improved ways of covering the game. The image-capture quality of cameras has increased, allowing crystal-clear slow-motion replays of even the fastest action. Cameras have also shrunk in size, so they can now be fitted into the back of the goal and other unusual places. The arrival of subscription and pay-per-view television via cable or satellite means that fans have to pay larger sums to watch chosen games, but in return more viewing options are being provided. Instant replays and different camera angles can be selected, and game statistics can also be accessed, just by pressing buttons on a remote control.

▲ *Fieldside cameras help viewers feel even closer to the action and their heroes.*

◀ *Up in the commentary boxes, commentators call the game, explaining the action on the field.*

Other media

Although in Europe television dominates, many fans in other countries rely on other forms of media to follow games. In most of the world fans can listen to live radio commentaries, just like listening to a baseball game in the U.S. In other countries, including the U.S., fans can keep up-to-date with results via the Internet. The net has thousands of official and unofficial websites dedicated to teams, competitions, and individual players.

▼ *France manager Didier Deschamps speaks to reporters about his team selection before the 2018 World Cup final.*

ENG | 1 | 2 | USA | 80:26

VAR

▲ *Giant screens show replays of goals and VAR (video assistant referee) reviews to fans at the game.*

The press conference

In countries where soccer is popular the players, manager, or chairman of the team frequently hold press conferences. This allows newspaper, TV, radio, and Internet reporters to have the latest information on transfers, new appointments, and resignations—not to mention opinions on game results—to share with the fans.

Stadiums

Just a place for spectators to watch soccer? Think again. Stadiums—particularly in Europe and South America—are the temples of soccer and each has its own special atmosphere and unique history.

▲ Opened in 1903, Hampden Park was home to the world's biggest crowds for the first half of the 1900s. The stadium underwent major refurbishment in the 1970s and 1990s.

Hampden Park [Scotland]

One of the first great stadiums, the home of the Scottish national team is also used by the Queens Park team. Until the 1950s, Hampden Park was the largest-capacity soccer arena in the world. The 149,415 people who watched Scotland play England in 1937 is still the U.K.'s official record attendance. It was refurbished into an all-seater stadium with a capacity of 52,000 and hosted some group games at the 2012 Olympic Games.

▼ The Maracana, also known as the Estadio Mario Filho, held the final of the 2014 World Cup and now seats 78,838 spectators.

▼ The new Wembley stadium opened in 2007 as a 90,000-capacity arena, with every seat covered. Its centerpiece is a giant, 436-ft. high arch.

Wembley [England]

Built in only 300 days in 1923, the twin towers of north London's Wembley stadium were a stirring sight for visiting fans for more than 75 years. Wembley has been the home of the England national team, the FA Cup final, and, perhaps most famously of all, host of England's 1966 World Cup final triumph. The original stadium was closed in 2000 and replaced by a state-of-the-art arena seven years later.

San Siro [Italy]

The Giuseppe Meazza stadium, better known as the San Siro, is home to two Italian Serie A giants. The San Siro started life in 1926 as the 35,000-capacity home of AC Milan. Milanese rivals Internazionale left their own stadium, Arena, to make the San Siro their home in 1955. The 85,000-seat ground has hosted one Champions League and two European Cup finals and games at the 1934 and 1990 World Cups.

▲ The 1990 renovations to the San Siro cost more than $75 million and added a third tier level of seats to the stadium, supported by 11 massive cylindrical towers.

Maracana (Brazil)

Based in Rio de Janeiro, Brazil, and home of the Brazilian national side, the Maracana is a huge arena. Opened in 1950 for the World Cup finals, the stadium holds the official world record attendance when 199,854 spectators came to see Brazil play Uruguay. It also holds the world record local professional team attendance of 177,656 for a game played in 1963 between Brazilian sides Flamingo and Fluminense.

▲ Home to one of the world's biggest teams, FC Barcelona, the Nou Camp, which means "the new ground," hosted the opening of the 1982 World Cup.

Nou Camp (Spain)

The magnificent home stadium of Spanish team Barcelona, the Nou Camp was opened in 1957 with a 90,000 capacity. This was later increased to a maximum capacity of around 115,000, but today stands at just below 99,000. Uniquely, the Nou Camp is connected via a walkway to a 16,500-seat stadium. This smaller stadium is where Barcelona's reserve or nursery team plays in the lower divisions of the Spanish competition.

Stade de France (France)

Built specifically for the 1998 World Cup finals, the Stade de France is a state-of-the-art sports stadium. Le Grand Stade, as it is popularly known, features a retractable lower level, 36 elevators, 43 cafés and snack bars, 670 bathrooms, 17 stores, and 454 floodlights. Built at a cost of more than $400 million, the stadium holds up to 80,000 spectators.

▼ The first competitive goal at Germany's Allianz Arena was scored by Bayern Munich's Owen Hargreaves in 2005.

► This view of the Stade de France was taken before the 2006 UEFA Champions League final between Barcelona and Arsenal. Barcelona won 2–1.

Allianz Arena (Germany)

The Allianz Arena is home to two Munich-based clubs, Bayern Munich and TSV 1860 Munich. It opened in 2005 and, with a capacity of just under 70,000, hosted six games at the following year's World Cup. International tournaments such as the World Cup provide a major impetus to build new stadiums and renovate older ones.

Great Competitions

Hundreds of different competitions, from youth five-on-five events to international tournaments for professionals, take place worldwide. Many competitions feature the best national or local teams all vying for a highly prestigious trophy.

▲ *Uruguay win the first ever World Cup.*

◀ *Maradona, clutching the 1986 World Cup, is held up by Argentina fans, while Kylian Mbappé (far left) celebrates with the trophy after the 2018 final against Croatia. France won 4-2.*

▲ *French forward Kylian Mbappé*

World Cup

The biggest soccer competition of them all, the FIFA World Cup was the brainchild of Frenchman Jules Rimet. Since 1930, the World Cup has provided a global stage for the national teams that make it through qualifying. This procedure sees more than 200 nations play in groups for the right to attend the finals. Only eight teams have won the World Cup—Brazil (five times), Italy and Germany (four times), Argentina, France, and Uruguay (twice), and England and Spain (once). The FIFA Women's World Cup was first held in 1991, with the U.S. winning four of the eight tournaments.

National leagues and continental competitions

Almost every soccer-playing country has its own national league made up of a number of professional teams competing against each other for the league title. Some of the world's most famous and competitive leagues include the German Bundesliga, the Spanish La Liga, the Italian Serie A, and the English Premier League. The best-placed teams in many countries' leagues often enter a continent-wide team competition, such as Europe's UEFA Champions League or South America's Copa Libertadores. Continental competitions also exist for national teams. The biggest of these, the European Championships, was first played in 1960. The current champions are Portugal, who won 1-0 against France in 2016. Portugal also won the very first UEFA Nations League title, with a 1-0 win over the Netherlands in 2019.

◀ *Germany's Jerome Boateng (left) battles with Cristiano Ronaldo for the ball at Euro 2012.*

▼ *Chilean players celebrate with the Copa America trophy after they won the competition for the first time in 2015, beating Argentina in the final.*

Copa America

The first continental competition for national teams began in 1910 and was named the Copa America—the South American Championship. A mere 8,000 spectators watched Argentina beat fierce rival Uruguay 4-1 in the final. Uruguay took their revenge in the second competition, held six years later in 1916, as they defeated Argentina to lift the trophy. Between 1959 and 1987, the tournament was usually played once every four years. In the years on both sides of these dates the tournament tended to take place every two years. Uruguay and Argentina head the list of champions, with 15 and 14 wins each. Chile, Peru, Paraguay, and Bolivia have also been winners. Brazil is the current cup holder, winning for the ninth time in 2019.

African Nations Cup

The African Nations Cup started in 1957 with just three teams—Egypt, Ethiopia, and Sudan. Egypt emerged as the winner. Since its small-scale beginnings, the competition has grown in size and importance. South Africa was readmitted into African soccer in 1992, and in 1996 the number of teams contesting the trophy was increased from 12 to 16. Fourteen different nations have won the tournament. Cameroon claimed two cups in a row in 2000 and 2002, Tunisia's first victory came in 2004, while Egypt triumphed in 2006, 2008, and 2010. Egypt have the most titles—seven—but the current holders are Algeria, who won in 2019.

▲ Riyad Mahrez holds the African Nations Cup high after Algeria won in 2019, its first title since 1990.

▲ Australia celebrates winning its first ever AFC Asian Cup, beating South Korea in the 2015 final.

Asian Cup

The Asian Cup started in 1956 and has boomed in quality and popularity since its early days. The 12 founder teams of the Asian Football Confederation have now expanded to some 45 countries—home to more than half of the world's soccer-playing peoples. Recent tournaments have involved major tussles between Far Eastern nations, such as China and Japan, and teams from the Middle East, such as Kuwait, United Arab Emirates, and Iran. The 2019 Asian Cup final saw Qatar win the trophy for the first time, beating Japan 3–1 in the final.

▲ Alex Morgan (right) of the U.S. and Japan's Nahomi Kawasumi at the 2012 Olympics.

▶ Mexico celebrates becoming Olympic football champions in 2012 after beating Brazil 2–1 in the final.

Olympic Games

Soccer was played at the first modern Olympics, held in 1896. Until the World Cup arrived in 1930, it was the only global soccer competition. From 1952 to 1988, all winners (except France in 1984) came from Eastern Europe. The 1990s saw the emergence of African soccer, with Nigeria and Cameroon winning in 1996 and 2000. Argentina claimed gold in 2004 and 2008, Mexico in 2012, and Brazil in 2016. Women's soccer first appeared at the 1996 Games, and the U.S. has a proud record, winning gold in 1996, 2004, 2008, and 2012. Germany won Olympic gold in 2016.

▼ Mexico celebrates winning its tenth CONCACAF Gold Cup in 2015, defeating Jamaica in the final.

CONCACAF Gold Cup

In 1941 a tournament for the soccer-playing countries of Central America was devised. Now known as the CONCACAF Gold Cup, it has been held in various formats and has occasionally involved invited guest teams such as Brazil. At times teams from North and South America have been included as well. In 1991, for example, the U.S. recorded its first victory in the competition, beating Honduras in the final, while Canada beat South American team Colombia in 2000, recording its first international tournament win since the 1904 Olympics. Mexico dominated the 1990s, winning three cups in a row between 1993 and 1998. In the 21st century, the U.S. and Mexico have been the top teams in the competition, each winning the trophy five times since 2002. Mexico is the current cup holder, beating the U.S. 1–0 in 2019.

Great Games 1

England 3, Hungary 6, friendly, 1953

Despite England's lackluster performance in the 1950 World Cup (the first time they entered the competition), many people still believed they were one of the best teams in the world. A friendly match at Wembley against a gifted and tactically brilliant Hungarian side, headed by the attacking genius of Ferenc Puskás, quickly shattered that illusion.

◀ *An England cross is cut out by Hungarian goalkeeper Gyula Grosics.*

▲ *Hungary's number ten, Ferenc Puskás, turns to the crowd to celebrate another goal for his team.*

Magic Magyars

From the first minute, the England side, boasting stars such as Stanley Matthews, Billy Wright, and Tom Finney, were outclassed and outplayed. The fluid Hungarian side, dubbed the "Magic Magyars," launched wave after wave of ferocious attacks. The rigid English tactics couldn't handle the sublime skills and movement of Kocsis and Puskás or those of the midfielder Nándor Hidegkuti, who scored a hat trick.

◀ *Nándor Hidegkuti (left) scores his third—and Hungary's sixth—goal. His first goal was scored in the first minute of the game.*

A class act

If Hungary hadn't eased up in the last 20 minutes of the game, the six goals they scored against England might have reached double figures. The Hungarian victory at Wembley was no fluke. Six months later an England side with seven changes travelled to Hungary for a re-match. England were thumped 7-1.

Real Madrid [Spain] 7, Eintracht Frankfurt [Germany] 3. European Cup Final, 1960

One of the finest exhibitions of soccer ever seen between two teams hell bent on winning the European Cup was watched by 127,621 people at Hampden Park in Glasgow, Scotland. Eintracht Frankfurt who had demolished their semifinal opponents Glasgow Rangers, opened the scoring and dominated the first quarter of the game. Real Madrid then burst into life with their two outstanding players Alfredo Di Stéfano and Puskás running rings around the German team. The great vision, swift movement, and superlative ball skills captivated the crowd and took Real Madrid from one goal down to 7-3 in style. Di Stéfano completed his hat trick in the 74th minute, just two minutes after Puskás had hit his fourth goal.

◀ *Puskás scores Real Madrid's fourth goal with an effortless kick from the penalty spot.*

▲ *The Real Madrid team pose for a photo before playing in the final of the 1960 European Cup.*

Non-stop action

Eintracht's commitment to attacking was as much a factor in this spellbinding match as the Spanish team's dazzling play. The Germans didn't give up easily—in the second half they hit the goalposts twice and twice put the ball in the back of the net. But it wasn't enough to prevent Real Madrid's onslaught.

◄ *Alfredo Di Stéfano scores Real Madrid's first goal in the 27th minute of this epic game.*

Pelé scores first

Pelé opened the Brazilian account with a superbly taken header in the 19th minute. But a sloppy Brazilian backpass was exploited by Boninsegna who equalized for Italy. In the second half Gérson put Brazil ahead again with a superlative individual effort. Picking up the ball 115 feet from goal, he changed direction to beat one defender before unleashing a precise and devastating shot.

Brazil 4, Italy 1. World Cup final, 1970

The 1970 World Cup in Mexico, the first to feature red and yellow cards and substitutes, was a wonderful display of high-class soccer and epic games. It culminated in a final that saw what is considered the finest team display by an international side. That side was Brazil. Their opponents, Italy, were on top form as well. Although Italy had beaten the West German side in the semifinals 4-3, the talents of, among others, Pelé, Rivellino, and Jairzinho proved just too much for them.

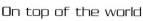

◄ *Italy's striker Luigi Riva is chased down by Brazilian central defender Brito who was involved in a sensational eight-player move for Brazil's fourth goal.*

◄ *Carlos Alberto celebrates scoring Brazil's fourth goal. Alberto captained the team during the 1970 World Cup.*

On top of the world

The remainder of the second half was a one-sided display of outstanding soccer, with the Brazilians dominating the game and scoring twice more. The final goal was pure genius. With five minutes to go, a wonderful series of passes by the Brazilian forwards resulted in Pelé rolling the ball out to his right. Timing his run to perfection, Carlos Alberto connected with the ball first time, thundering a shot into the Italian net. It was a fitting climax to the game. Satellite broadcasting, used for the first time during this World Cup, allowed millions of people around the world to watch one of the greatest of all international games.

▲ *Jairzinho runs away from goal celebrating after scoring Brazil's third goal. He became the first player to score in every round of a World Cup tournament.*

Great Games 2

Congo 3, Mali 2. African Nations Cup final, 1972

Soccer in Africa is not a recent phenomenon. Although the World Cup and Olympic exploits of teams such as Nigeria and Cameroon during the 1990s are well known, African soccer has a long history. The African Nations Cup, which started in 1957 and is the equivalent of the European Championships, has produced some classic games. One of the greatest is the 1972 final, held in Cameroon, between two very strong sides—Congo and Mali.

▲ François M'Pelé, who scored for Congo in the final, played for the French side Paris St. Germain during the 1970s.

▲ A Mali defender wins a challenge for the ball with M'Pelé. As runners up this remains Mali's highest achievement to date in the African Nations Cup.

No let up

Mali dominated the first half. Only a series of acrobatic saves from Congo goalkeeper Masima kept Mali at bay, although they managed to take the lead right at the end of the first half. Congo surged forward in the second half with M'Bono scoring two goals in two minutes. M'Pelé added a third, and the game looked over until Mali scored their second with 15 minutes to go. Despite a grandstand finish with both sides playing wonderfully fluid soccer, the score remained 3–2 to Congo.

West Germany 2, Holland 1. World Cup final, 1974

Although billed as a battle between Dutch maestro Johan Cruyff and brilliant German tactician Franz Beckenbauer, the game was in fact a fascinating and highly-skilled encounter between two teams at their peak. The game began explosively, with Cruyff brought down in the German penalty area soon after kickoff. The penalty was converted by Johan Neeskens. The Dutch continued to dominate the game with elegant and fluid movement focused around Cruyff, Neeskens, and Johnny Rep.

▲ West German goalkeeper Sepp Maier catches the ball in front of Dutch forward Johan Cruyff. The West German victory was its second World Cup title, coming 20 years after West Germany's first win over Hungary in 1954 in Bern.

Enter "Der Bomber"

Superb defending and outstanding goalkeeping from Sepp Maier prevented Holland from netting the vital second goal. The Germans made the Dutch pay for their lack of killer instinct by equalizing with a penalty. Then, in the 43rd minute, the German striker Gerd Müller, nicknamed "Der Bomber," scored a second for his team with a glorious individual effort.

Dutch pressure

The Dutch pressed furiously for an equalizer, but Sepp Maier, the goalkeeper of the tournament, continued to thwart them. As more space opened up, West Germany also had their chances—with Müller particularly unlucky when he had a goal disallowed for offside, although replays confirmed he was onside.

▶ Despite giving away a penalty, West Germany and Bayern Munich forward Uli Hoeness, just 22 years old at the time, played an important part in the German victory.

Revenge

The 2–1 final scoreline meant that West Germany were crowned world champions. Unfortunately for the Dutch fans and players, they had to wait 14 years for victory over the Germans. Their Euro '88 side, boasting legendary players such as Ruud Gullit and Marco van Basten, finally put to rest painful memories of their 1974 World Cup loss.

◀ Gerd Müller hits a powerful low shot past Dutch defender Ruud Krol to score West Germany's winner. It would be the last goal for the clinical striker who notched 68 goals for his country in only 62 games.

▶ French midfielder Alain Giresse (right) formed a magnificent partnership with Jean Tigana, Luis Fernández, and Michel Platini throughout the tournament.

France 3, Portugal 2. European Championships, 1984

This enthralling semifinal was the game that put the European Championships on the map. The French midfield of Jean Tigana, Alain Giresse, and Michel Platini controlled much of the match with a wonderful display of passing and movement. At halftime, the much-favored French team were 1–0 up thanks to Jean-François Domergue. During the second half, the French couldn't consolidate their lead. Attack after attack was repelled with the Portuguese goalkeeper Manuel Bento making some great saves. Then in the 73rd minute Rui Jordão equalized for Portugal, shocking the 55,000 crowd packed into Marseille's Velodrome stadium.

▶ Michel Platini controls and shields the ball from a Portuguese defender during the game. Platini's haul of nine goals in the tournament remains a European Championships record.

▲ French defender Maxime Bossis falls to the ground. The French victory in the finals helped ease memories of Bossis' missed penalty, which had lost France their World Cup semifinal against West Germany two years earlier.

At the last minute

Extra time came and the game opened up further with wave after wave of attacks by both sides. Portugal took the lead with striker Jordao scoring again, but France pulled back with a goal from Domergue. Another dreaded penalty shootout looked inevitable. Then in the very last minute of extra time Jean Tigana played a cross into the penalty area. It was met by Platini who struck it sweetly into the back of the net, securing victory seconds before the final whistle. Four days later, France beat Spain in the final 2–0 to win their first-ever international competition. Platini was made player of the tournament.

Great Games 3

Argentina 2, Nigeria 3. Olympic final, 1996

Inspired attacking from both sides made for a thrilling match, full of goalmouth incidents. The game began badly for Nigeria. With less than two minutes on the clock, poor defending allowed Argentina's Claudio Lopez plenty of space to head home the opening goal. But Nigeria weren't a team to give up easily. In a dramatic semifinal against Brazil they had come from behind to beat the South Americans 4–3, and now in the final they fought back with great determination and flair.

▲ *Ariel Ortega is fouled by Nigeria's Taribo West resulting in a penalty—and Argentina's second goal of the game.*

▲ *The Nigerian team form a huddle before kickoff in the final. The Super Eagles' victory would see them become the first team from Africa to win gold at the Olympics.*

On the attack

Celestine Babayaro's equalizing header was as impressive as his celebration—a spectacular double somersault. However, the Argentinians struck back with a penalty taken by Hernan Crespo. With 15 minutes to go, Amokachi latched on to the ball and flicked it over the Argentinian goalkeeper. The final appeared to be heading for extra time when Nigeria was awarded a free kick wide out on the left.

Going for gold

The Argentinian defense tried to catch Nigeria offside, but Emmanuel Amunike beat the trap and volleyed home the winning goal in the 89th minute. The final whistle was met with wild celebrations. Nigeria had become the first African nation to win a major international cup competition.

◄ *Nigeria's powerful forward Daniel Amokachi competes for the ball against Argentina's Roberto Sensini. Amokachi scored Nigeria's second goal in the 74th minute.*

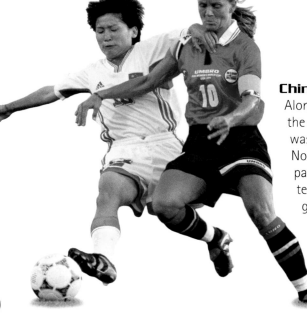

China 5, Norway 0. Women's World Cup semifinal, 1999

Along with the eventual winners—U.S.—Norway and China were far and away the most-favored sides in the 1999 World Cup finals. This semifinal clash was a contrast in styles between the determined and defensively strong Norwegian team and a Chinese side that relied on speed and close-range passing. China ran riot. The blistering speed and superb movement of their team proved far too much for a tough Norwegian side, who started the game as favorites in many commentators' eyes. China made a fairytale start to the game when striker Sun Wen scored in the third minute.

◄ *Ying Liu, one of China's talented strikers, shows she's equally adept at defending as she makes a robust sliding challenge on the veteran Norwegian captain Linda Medalen.*

Unstoppable

Liu Ailing doubled the lead with a blistering right-footed volley 11 minutes later. Ailing, superb with either foot, scored her second, a left-footed volley, after a corner wasn't properly cleared by the Norwegian defense. Norway threatened the Chinese goal on a number of occasions in the second half but one of the best goalkeepers in the women's game, Gao Hong, pulled off three spectacular saves to foil them. China retaliated with a fourth goal in the 63rd minute from yet another volley, this time by defender Fan Yunjie. Sun Wen's 72nd-minute penalty made her joint top scorer for the tournament, along with the Brazilian Sissi, and completed the 5-0 victory, equalling Norway's worst ever defeat.

▲ *The Chinese players celebrate another goal in their devastating 5–0 victory over Norway.*

▼ *Attacker Ismael Urzaiz celebrates after Spain manages to hold on for a narrow win in an epic game.*

▲ *Yugoslavia's Dragan Stojkovic competes for the ball against Iván Helguera.*

▲ *Spain's Pep Guardiola (center) is beaten to a high ball by Slobodan Komljenovic.*

Spain 4, Yugoslavia 3. Euro 2000

This pulsating Euro 2000 game started with Spain looking the sharper team, taking out a number of chances. But Spain was hit by a classic counterattack that saw Savo Miloševic head home for Yugoslavia. Spain pressed forward in numbers, and Raul's darting run let Alfonso tie. Halftime substitute Dejan Govedarica took only six minutes to restore Yugoslavia's lead with a superb strike from the edge of the penalty area. Yet just one minute later, Miguel Salgado fired in a wonderful curling shot to tie.

> *"The difference between heaven and hell is one minute."*
>
> Josep Guardiola after the Spain vs. Yugoslavia match.

Late heartbreak

With the game poised at 2–2, it appeared that the turning point had come in the 63rd minute when Jokanovic was sent off. Spain now held the advantage, yet it was ten-man Yugoslavia who went ahead. A disputed injury-time penalty for Spain seemed to have created the fairest result—a fabulous 3–3 tie—but more drama was to come, with Alfonso volleying home a last-gasp winning goal for Spain.

Liverpool 4, Barcelona 0. Champions League, 2019

May 2019 saw an epic Champions League comeback as two legendary teams battled in the second leg of the semifinals. Barcelona held a 3–0 lead from the first leg, and few fans gave Liverpool much hope of clawing back the deficit. But the Reds tore into their Spanish opponents, and a goal from Divock Origi in the seventh minute gave them hope. Barcelona couldn't handle Liverpool's non-stop, all-action play, and two goals in two minutes from substitute Georginio Wijnaldum after half-time tied the match 3–3. And when Origi struck the winner in the 78th minute, Anfield erupted on one of the most sensational nights in the history of this famous stadium. In an all-English final against Tottenham, Liverpool lifted their sixth European Cup, a record for an English club.

▼ *Liverpool's Belgian forward Divock Origi controls the ball under pressure from Sergio Busquets and Sergi Roberto.*

The Great Players I

Alfredo Di Stéfano [born 1926, Buenos Aires, Argentina. Died 2014]
Di Stéfano (right) joined his father's old team, River Plate, as a teenager and soon became part of an extremely successful forward line known as "La Maquina"—The Machine. In 1953 he moved to the legendary Spanish team Real Madrid, which dominated European soccer in the 1950s and early 1960s. A center-forward, Di Stéfano was also brilliant at defending, tackling, creating chances for other players, as well as scoring many superbly taken goals himself. Real Madrid player and coach Miguel Munoz summed up his contribution to the game—"The greatness of Di Stéfano was that with him in your side you had two players in every position."

Lev Yashin [born 1929, Moscow, former Soviet Union. Died 1990]
Just slightly better than Gordon Banks, Lev Yashin (left) is still regarded as soccer's greatest goalkeeper. Nicknamed the "Black Panther" for his incredible agility and awesome saves, he had an almost supernatural anticipation of where the ball would next appear. During his 20-year career at Moscow Dynamo (where he had originally started out as the team's hockey goaltender) the team won the Supreme League title six times and the Soviet Cup twice. He also won 78 caps for the Soviet Union. Records are sketchy, but Yashin is believed to have saved more than 150 penalties in his illustrious career. In 1968 he was awarded the Order of Lenin, at that time the Soviet Union's highest honor.

Pelé [Edson Arantes do Nascimento, born 1940, Tres Coracoes, Brazil]
If any player deserved a ten out of ten over a long career, it has to be the man who always wore that number for his main team, Santos, and for his national team, Brazil. Pelé had it all—speed, strength, creativity, breathtaking vision, and skills to match it all. At the age of 17 he became an instant celebrity, scoring six goals for Brazil's 1958 World-Cup-winning team. It was the first of three World Cups that Pelé helped to win for his country. The last, in 1970, featured some of his finest moments— outrageous fakes, flicks, passes, and shots few others would have attempted. Pelé played 93 internationals for Brazil, with a remarkable tally of 77 goals. When Pelé retired from Santos in 1974 after 18 years, the team removed the number ten shirt from their team as a tribute. He later came out of retirement to help promote professional soccer in the United States, playing for the New York Cosmos before retiring for good in 1977. In 1994 Pelé was appointed Brazil's Minister of Sport.

Eusébio da Silva Ferreira (born 1942, Lourenco Marques, Mozambique. Died 2014)

Eusébio played his early soccer in Mozambique, at that time a Portuguese colony. Although groomed to play for the famous Portuguese team Sporting Lisbon, he was snapped up by their great rival Benfica. He scored more than 300 goals in his 15-year career at Benfica, and the team won major honors in all but two of those years. Blessed with an explosive right foot, Eusébio was wonderfully skilled in all areas of attacking play. He was admired for his sportsmanship, too, even in the tensest encounters. In 1965 he was voted European Footballer (soccer player) of the Year. The following year, Eusébio was the leading scorer in the World Cup with nine goals.

Franz Beckenbauer

(born 1945, Munich, Germany)

An outstanding defender, Beckenbauer revolutionized the position of sweeper. Originally the sweeper was an ultradefensive position, but he made it into an exciting way of turning defense into attack. In game after game for Bayern Munich and his national side, West Germany, the player nicknamed "Kaiser Franz" had a game-winning impact, creating hundreds of scoring opportunities for his teammates. He didn't hold back from making shots on goal himself and put away 44 goals for Bayern. Beckenbauer was capped 103 times for West Germany, and under his captaincy, the team triumphed in the 1974 World Cup. He was appointed manager of the national team in 1984 and steered them to victory over Argentina in the 1990 World Cup final.

George Best (born 1946, Belfast, Northern Ireland. Died 2005)

One of the most extravagantly gifted players to grace the game, George Best shared with Pelé attacking vision, brilliant goal scoring skills, and an eye for the unexpected or outrageous. Superb with both feet and a fearless tackler, Best was a supreme dribbler of the ball. He was also a deadly finisher with 137 goals for England's Manchester United, the team he joined as a teenager. He was instrumental in United's European Cup victory over Benfica in 1968. His national side, Northern Ireland, never made it to the World Cup finals. Although he made a number of comebacks in both Britain and North America, the player dubbed "the fifth Beatle" was never the same after he sensationally quit Manchester United in 1973. The pressure of fame and being Britain's first soccer superstar had sadly taken its toll.

The Great Players 2

Johan Cruyff (born 1947, Amsterdam, Holland, Died 2016)
One of the greatest of European players, Cruyff (left) was a key player in the Dutch revolution known as "total football." This involved players changing positions with breathtaking speed and effectiveness. Cruyff, three times European Footballer of the Year, displayed sublime ball skills and, although a center-forward, he was equally effective in midfield or on the wings. He enjoyed huge success at the Dutch team Ajax, where he was instrumental in the team winning three European Cups. In 1973 he moved to Barcelona where he helped the Spanish team win a number of league and cup titles. Cruyff returned to Ajax and then Barcelona as manager, taking both teams to victory in European cup competitions.

Diego Maradona (born 1960, Buenos Aires, Argentina)
A superb goalscorer with beautiful technical skills, Maradona (right) was *the* player of the 1980s. Highlights of his career include winning two Italian league titles with Napoli and his performance in the 1986 World Cup, when he transformed a solid Argentinian side into the world's best. During the tournament Maradona provided a serious contender for the greatest goal ever—against England during the quarterfinals (earlier in the same game he infamously used his hand to score a goal). Despite leading Argentina to the 1990 World Cup finals, where they finished as runners-up after losing 1–0 to West Germany, Maradona's later years were sadly dogged by failed drug tests and disappointing comebacks.

Michel Platini (born 1955, Joeuf, France)
One of the most effective midfielders the game has ever seen, Platini (left) captained the French side to the 1982 World Cup semifinals and to victory in the 1984 European Championships. Supremely creative, Platini was dazzling in attack or hovering around the midfield, hitting deadly accurate 130-foot passes. Playing for the great Italian side Juventus, he was Serie A's leading scorer and was crowned European Footballer of the Year in 1983, 1984, and 1985. In 1992, five years after retiring, he became manager of the French national side and later headed France's successful bid to host the World Cup in 1998.

Cristiano Ronaldo (born 1985, Funchal, Portugal)

Lionel Messi's greatest rival is soccer's most famous face, Cristiano Ronaldo. His career took off in 2003 when Manchester United signed him from Lisbon-based club Sporting CP. During six seasons Ronaldo showcased his skills as a deadly winger who could score on demand and set up goals galore. He masterminded three Premier League titles and a Champions League win for the Red Devils. A move to Real Madrid in 2009 for more than $130 million made Ronaldo the world's most expensive player. This hat-trick hero has scored a record 34 La Liga hat-tricks and is the Champions League's top scorer. As captain of Portugal, Ronaldo led his team to their first major success at Euro 2016. Like Messi, Ronaldo has won the world's greatest player award five times.

Mariel Margaret "Mia" Hamm
(born 1972, Alabama, USA)

The most famous player in women's soccer, Mia Hamm was the youngest-ever American international when she debuted in 1987 at the age of 15. She dominated the 1990s as the game's most inspirational and devastating attacker, with 158 international goals to her credit, helping the U.S. win both Olympic and World Cup titles. She was voted U.S. soccer's Female Athlete of the Year an unprecedented five years in a row, from 1994 to 1998. In 2003 a third World Cup win was beyond the U.S. team, but Hamm could console herself with a second Olympic gold medal in 2004. She retired shortly afterward.

Lionel Messi (born 1987, Rosario, Argentina)

Living legend Lionel Messi grew up in Argentina before moving to Spain at the age of 13 years to join Barcelona. As a child, Messi was diagnosed with a growth hormone deficiency, but the Spanish club organized medical treatment to help him. Their investment paid off as the gifted teenager excelled in the youth academy before playing his first competitive game for Barcelona in 2004. He soon became captain for both his club and country, and has been breaking records ever since. The superstar striker scored 73 goals in a single season (2011–12) and in the following season he bagged goals in 21 consecutive league games. Messi is La Liga's top scorer, with more than 400 goals during 14 seasons at Barcelona. This glorious goalscoring record has resulted in nine La Liga and four Champions League titles. Messi's trophy cabinet is spilling over with five Ballon d'Or trophies for the world's greatest player.

Soccer History

Many fans from other countries are not aware that the United States boasts as long a soccer history as theirs—in some cases longer. From its origins in the 1600s, it has flourished into one of the nation's fastest-growing team sports and now features the first-ever professional league for women.

Early history

Soccer, or a very basic form of the game we know today, was brought over to the U.S. by British settlers in the 1600s. The early academic colleges of the northeastern United States occasionally played "soccer." For example, from 1827 onward classes at Harvard played a once-a-year contest that was closer to a crowd brawl than a real sport, so much so that the event became known as "Bloody Monday." As the game developed into a codified sport in Britain it started to be organized and played in the United States as well. The first team with a roster of players in the U.S. is believed to be the Oneida team. Based in Boston and playing from 1862 onward, it is considered to be the first organized soccer team outside of Great Britain.

"Football" was the name given to both the sports we know today as soccer and rugby. The kicking-only game became known as "association football," which was abbreviated as "assoc.," which led to "soccer"—the name that stayed in the U.S. Soccer was played in a number of colleges, but in the 1870s a split occured between soccer, football, and rugby. Soccer declined as a sport of privileged Americans. New immigrants to the U.S. kept the soccer flame alight, and by 1884 a group of ex-British soccer lovers formed the American Football Association. The AFA ran a cup competition, the American Cup, from 1885 to 1898 and also organized the first national side, which in 1885–86 played two games against Canada—the first a 1–0 defeat, the second, a 3–2 win.

In 1894 the first attempt was made to establish a completely professional soccer league. It came from a group of baseball team owners, looking for a way to fill their stadiums outside of the baseball season. The league didn't make it through an entire season. However, other leagues sprung up, including the National Association Football (soccer) League and the Southern New England Football (soccer) League.

In 1921 the American Soccer League was founded. The wealthier teams in other leagues, such as Bethlehem Steel and Fall River, left their own leagues that were struggling to attract big enough crowds, and joined the ASL. Backed by big business, the ASL was fully professional and started on a strong foot. Crowds often reached five figures, and in 1925 two additional teams—the New Bedford Whalers and the Boston Wonder Workers—joined. The Fall River Marksmen, founded by businessman Sam Mark, became one of the most dominant teams in U.S. soccer history. They won five championships in eight years and three cup competitions. Sam Mark aided this achievement by signing top players from Europe, particularly the U.K., such as Tec White, Charlie McGill, and Harold Brittan.

Although soccer was booming, disputes arose between the league, teams, and other authorities. By the time these were resolved the Wall Street crash had occurred and with it the onset of the Great Depression. The ASL never regained the heights it reached in the mid-1920s and disbanded in 1933. The second American Soccer League (ASL2) was started in 1933 with more modest aims and a completely new roster of teams. Based in New York, New Jersey, and Philadelphia, the league kept players at a semiprofessional level. The Kearny Scots was the first dominant team in the ASL2, winning five league titles in a row between 1937 and 1941.

A truly professional soccer league

In the boom years of the 1950s onward, sports participation and spectating rose like never before, partly due to increased leisure time and the rise of television. The ASL2 was still in existence, along with many amateur and some semiprofessional teams, but a brand-new professional league became a possibility. Two competing organizations were formed in the 1960s, both with the aim of establishing professional soccer as a major American sport—the United Soccer Association and the National Professional Soccer League. The two organizations argued over many things, including player transfers. Yet, neither attracted the necessary large TV audiences, and in 1968 they merged to form the North American Soccer League (NASL).

Of the first 17 teams in the NASL, only five were in business by the third season. All looked bleak until teams managed to attract enough local interest to keep going, and slowly new teams joined. The most notable of these was the New York Cosmos, who rocked the soccer world with their signing of the world's greatest player, Pelé, in 1975. Pelé's arrival saw huge media interest, attendances rocket, and more top players join the NASL, including Johan Cruyff, Franz Beckenbauer, and George Best. For a few short years, the NASL boasted the glamour of the international game, but the lack of a national TV deal and rising player costs would lead to the league's demise in 1984. Soccer, however, had made its mark on many

Americans as a fun, relatively safe sport to play and one that required little equipment.

U.S. national teams

There had been friendly games before, but the U.S. men's national team was not recognized by FIFA until 1916. The first officially sanctioned national team tied 1–1 with Norway and beat Sweden 3–2. After competing in the 1924 and 1928 Olympics, the U.S. national team was one of 13 nations to attend the first-ever World Cup, held in Uruguay in 1930. The U.S. team reached the semifinals, where they lost to Argentina. The team competed regularly in World Cup qualifiers and finals and in 1950 created one of the World Cup's greatest shocks, defeating England 1–0. Joe Gaetjens scored the winning goal.

The 1990s saw leading U.S. players plying their trade for teams in Europe, the U.S. winning the CONCACAF Championship in 1991, and three years later, the country hosting the World Cup finals tournament. Drawing a record 3.6 million spectators, and averaging 67,000 per game, the World Cup was considered a major success. The tournament featured plenty of attractive soccer, exciting games, and shocks, such as the U.S. beating favored Colombia, while American players like Claudio Reyna, Alexi Lalas, and Cobi Jones became household names.

The U.S. men's team was, by now, considered a serious opponent and a regular qualifier for World Cups. They reached the quarterfinals in the 2002 World Cup, entered the top ten of FIFA's world rankings the same year, and won repeated CONCACAF Gold Cups in 2002, 2005, 2007, 2013, and 2017. The team qualified for the 2014 World Cup but failed to reach the quarterfinals. The team were unsuccessful in qualifying for the 2018 World Cup in Russia.

The women's national team, only formed in 1985, quickly became a dominant force in international soccer. Inspired by talents such as Mia Hamm, Michelle Akers, Tiffany Melbricht, and Brandi Chastain, they won the first-ever Women's World Cup in 1991, repeated the feat in 1999, and won back-to-back titles in 2015 and 2019. In addition, they have won four Olympic Games soccer competitions, in 1996, 2004, 2008, and 2012, and ten Algarve Cups. The team now boasts exciting young talent, including Tierna Davidson, mixed with experienced veterans such as team co-captains Carli Lloyd, Alex Morgan, and Megan Rapinoe. They have also been credited with massively raising interest in soccer at both local and national levels. As a result, soccer has been the fastest-growing women's team sport in the U.S. for a number of years.

21st-century professional leagues

Buoyed by the excellence of U.S. women's soccer and by the massive success of the 1994 World Cup, the MLS was launched in 1995. The question was, could soccer work at a professional level in the U.S.? It had been more than ten years since a professional soccer league existed in the U.S., so did it stand a chance against the large array of other team sports present in the United States? Would it hook fans in large enough numbers, and would the press, radio, and, most important, television companies give it the necessary coverage and publicity for it to flourish? The answers for the first season, starting in 1996, were positive. Good public relations and the positive memories of World Cup 1994 saw just over three million spectators pay to see the games in the flesh, while many more watched games or followed the news and results on TV. Starting with ten teams, the 1998–1999 season saw the MLS grow to 12, as teams from Miami and Chicago joined. While several teams have come and gone, the MLS has gradually strengthened and increased in size, with its first Canadian-based team, Toronto FC, joining in 2007, the Seattle Sounders in 2009, New York City FC and Orlando City Soccer Club in 2015, and FC Cincinnati in 2019. The MLS currently has 24 teams, and hopes to continue growing.

Amid a great deal of fanfare, the first professional league for women's soccer in North America was launched in 2001. WUSA (the Women's United Soccer Association) was set up with eight teams and an operating budget of approximately $40 million. Top foreign players, especially from powerhouse nations like Brazil, Germany, and China, were recruited to play alongside U.S. players. Despite some success, WUSA's operations were suspended in 2003, after three seasons, due to debts. The operating budget was spent quickly, and the league had problems attracting major sponsors. However, the profile of women's soccer had been raised and was helped further by the switching of the 2003 Women's World Cup from China—where the SARS virus had struck—to the U.S.

With a WUSA reorganizing committee founding the Women's Soccer Initiative Inc. to establish women's professional soccer, it seemed only a matter of time before a second attempt at a women's professional league in North America would occur. This was launched as Women's Professional Soccer (WPS) in 2009, with seven teams in the first season and a further two teams, Atlanta Beat and Philadelphia Independence, joining in 2010. Top-class international players such as the Brazilians Cristiane and Marta (voted the Most Valuable Player of the first season), England's Kelly Smith, and Australia's Sarah Walsh joined leading U.S. players like Christie Rampone, Abby Wambach, and up-and-coming stars. The National Women's Soccer League (NWSL) began in 2013 with eight teams, four of which originally played in WPS. Nine teams play in 2019, and there are plans to expand to 14 teams in the coming years.

Stats and Facts

Statistics and records are a vital part of the game for fans, commentators, and even managers. Below is a selection of some of the most important and fascinating soccer stats available.

National Association Football (soccer) League (NAFL) winners

1895 Bayonne Centerville
1898 Paterson True Blues
1907 West Hudson
1908 Paterson Rangers
1909 Clark A. A.
1910 West Hudson
1911 Jersey A. C.
1912 West Hudson
1913 West Hudson
1914 Brooklyn F. C.
1915 West Hudson
1916 Alley Boys
1917 Jersey A. C.
1918 Paterson F. C.
1919 Bethlehem Steel
1920 Bethlehem Steel
1921 Bethlehem Steel

American Soccer League I (ASL1) champions

1922 Philadelphia FC
1923 J. & P. Coats
1924 Fall River Marksmen
1925 Fall River Marksmen
1926 Fall River Marksmen
1927 Bethlehem Steel
1928 Boston Wonder Workers
1929 Fall River Marksmen
1930 Fall River Marksmen
1931 New York Giants
1932 New Bedford Whalers
1933 Fall River FC

American Soccer League II (ASL2) champions

1934 Kearney Irish-Americans
1935 German-Americans
1936 New York Americans
1937 Scots-Americans
1938 Scots-Americans
1939 Newark Scots
1940 Newark Scots
1941 Newark Scots
1942 Philadelphia Americans
1943 Brooklyn Hispano
1944 Philadelphia Americans
1945 Brookhattan
1946 Baltimore Americans
1947 Philadelphia Americans
1948 Philadelphia Americans
1949 Philadelphia Nationals
1950 Philadelphia Nationals
1951 Philadelphia Nationals
1952 Philadelphia Americans
1953 Philadelphia Nationals
1954 New York Americans
1955 Uhrik Truckers (Philadelphia)
1956 Uhrik Truckers (Philadelphia)
1957 New York Hakoah
1958 New York Hakoah
1959 New York Hakoah
1960 Colombo
1961 Ukrainian Nationals (Philadelphia)
1962 Ukrainian Nationals (Philadelphia)
1963 Ukrainian Nationals (Philadelphia)
1964 Ukrainian Nationals (Philadelphia)
1965 Hartford Football Club
1966 Roma Soccer Club
1967 Baltimore St. Gerards
1968 Ukrainian Nationals (Philadelphia)
1968 Washington Darts
1969 Washington Darts
1970 Ukrainian Nationals (Philadelphia)
1971 New York Greeks
1972 Cincinnati Comets
1973 New York Apollo
1974 Rhode Island Oceaneers
1975 New York Apollo
1976 Los Angeles Skyhawks
1977 New Jersey Americans
1978 New York Apollo
1979 Sacramento Gold
1980 Pennsylvania Stoners
1981 Carolina Lightnin'
1982 Detroit Express
1983 Jacksonville Tea Men

North American Soccer League (NASL) winners

1967 Oakland Clippers
1967 Los Angeles Wolves
1968 Atlanta Chiefs
1969 Kansas City Spurs
1970 Rochester Lancers
1971 Dallas Tornado
1972 New York Cosmos
1973 Philadelphia Atoms
1974 Los Angeles Aztecs
1975 Tampa Bay Rowdies
1976 Toronto Metros-Croatia
1977 New York Cosmos
1978 New York Cosmos
1979 Vancouver Whitecaps
1980 New York Cosmos
1981 Chicago Sting
1982 New York Cosmos
1983 Tulsa Roughnecks
1984 Chicago Sting

National Professional Soccer League winners

1992 Detroit Rockers
1993 Kansas City Attack
1994 Cleveland Crunch
1995 St. Louis Ambush
1996 Cleveland Crunch
1997 Kansas City Attack
1998 Milwaukee Wave
1999 Cleveland Crunch
2000 Milwaukee Wave
2001 Milwaukee Wave

Major League Soccer (MLS) Cup winners

2000 Kansas City Wizards
2001 San Jose Earthquakes
2002 Los Angeles Galaxy
2003 San Jose Earthquakes
2004 D. C. United
2005 Los Angeles Galaxy
2006 Houston Dynamo
2007 Houston Dynamo
2008 Columbus Crew
2009 Real Salt Lake
2010 Colorado Rapids
2011 Los Angeles Galaxy
2012 Los Angeles Galaxy
2013 Sporting Kansas City
2014 Los Angeles Galaxy
2015 Portland Timbers
2016 Seattle Sounders FC
2017 Toronto FC
2018 Atlanta United FC

U.S. Open Cup Championship games

Listed are the results since 1950. In some seasons the competition was played over two games. The score of the second game is in parentheses.

1950 St. Louis Simpkins-Ford 2 (1), Fall River Ponta Delgada 0 (1)
1951 New York German-Hungarian 2 (6), Pittsburgh Heidelberg 4 (2)
1952 Pittsburgh Hamarville 3 (4), Philadelphia Nationals 4 (1)
1953 Chicago Falcons 2 (1), Pittsburgh Hamarville 0 (1)
1954 New York Americans 1 (2), St. Louis Kutis 0 (0)
1955 S. C. Eintracht 2, Los Angeles Danish Americans 0
1956 Pittsburgh Hamarville 0 (3), Chicago Schwaben 1 (1)
1957 St. Louis Kutis 3 (3), New York Hakoah 0 (1)
1958 Los Angeles Kickers 2, Baltimore Pompei 1
1959 San Pedro McIlvane Canvasbacks 4, Fall River SC 3
1960 Philadelphia Ukrainian Nationals 5, Los Angeles Kickers 3
1961 Philadelphia Ukrainian Nationals 2 (5), Los Angeles Scots 2 (2)

1962 New York Hungarians 3, San Francisco Scots 2
1963 Philadelphia Ukrainian Nationals 1, Los Angeles Armenian 0
1964 Los Angeles Kickers 2 (2), Philadelphia Ukrainian Nationals 2 (0)
1965 New York Ukrainians 1 (3), Chicago Hansa 1 (0)
1966 Philadelphia Ukrainian Nationals 1 (3), Orange County 0 (0)
1967 New York Greek-American 4, Orange County 2
1968 New York Greek-American 1 (1), Chicago Olympic 1 (0)
1969 New York Greek-American 1, Montabello Armenians 0
1970 S. C. Elizabeth 2, Los Angeles Croatia 1
1971 New York Hota 6, San Pedro Yugoslavs 4
1972 S. C. Elizabeth 1, San Pedro Yugoslavs 0
1973 Los Angeles Maccabee 5, Cleveland Inter 3
1974 New York Greek-American 2, Chicago Croatia 0
1975 LA Maccabee 1, New York Inter-Giuliana 0
1976 San Francisco A. C. 1, New York Inter-Giuliana 0
1977 Los Angeles Maccabee 5, Philadelphia United German-Hungarian 1
1978 Los Angeles Maccabee 2, Bridgeport Vasco de Gama 0
1979 Brooklyn Dodgers 2, Chicago Croatian 1
1980 New York Pancyprian Freedoms 3, Los Angeles Maccabee 2
1981 Los Angeles Maccabee 5, Brooklyn Dodgers 1
1982 New York Pancyprian Freedoms 4, Los Angeles Maccabee 3
1983 New York Pancyprian Freedoms 4, St. Louis Kutis 3

1984 New York A. O. Krete 4, Chicago Croatian 2
1985 San Francisco Greek-American A. C. 2, St. Louis Kutis 1
1986 St. Louis Kutis 1, San Pedro Yugoslavs 0
1987 Washington Club Espana 1, Seattle Eagles 0
1988 St. Louis Busch Seniors 1, San Francisco Greek-American 0
1989 St. Petersburg Kickers 2, New York Greek-American/Atlas 1
1990 Chicago A.A.C. Eagles 2, Brooklyn Italians 1
1991 Brooklyn Italians 1, Richardson Rockets 0
1992 San Jose Oaks 2, Bridgeport Vasco de Gama 1
1993 San Francisco CD Mexico 5, Philadelphia United German-Hungarians 0
1994 San Francisco Greek-American 3, Milwaukee Bavarian Leinenkugel 0
1995 Richmond Kickers 1, El Paso Patriots 1 (pens 4-2)
1996 Washington D. C. United 3, Rochester Rhinos (A-League) 0
1997 Dallas Burn 0, Washington D.C. United 0, (penalties 5-3)
1998 Chicago Fire 2, Columbus Crew 1
1999 Rochester Ragin' Rhinos 2, Colorado Rapids 0
2000 Chicago Fire 2, Miami Fusion 1
2001 Los Angeles Galaxy 2, New England Revolution 1
2002 Columbus Crew 1, Los Angeles Galaxy 0
2003 Chicago Fire 1, NY/NJ MetroStars 0
2004 Kansas City Wizards 1, Chicago Fire 0
2005 Los Angeles Galaxy 1, F. C. Dallas 0
2006 Chicago Fire 3, Los Angeles Galaxy 1
2007 New England Revolution 3, F. C. Dallas 2

2008 D.C. United 2, Charleston Battery 1
2009 Seattle Sounders 2, D.C. United 1
2010 Seattle Sounders 2, Columbus Crew 1
2011 Seattle Sounders 2, Chicago Fire 0
2012 Sporting Kansas City 1, Seattle Sounders 1 (pens 3-2)
2013 D.C. United 1, Real Salt Lake 0
2014 Seattle Sounders 3, Philadelphia Union 1
2015 Sporting Kansas City 1, Philadelphia Union 1 (pens 7-6)
2016 FC Dallas 4, New England Revolution 2
2017 Sporting Kansas City 2, New York Red Bulls 1
2018 Houston Dynamo 3, Philadelphia Union 0

Women's Professional Soccer (WPS) playoff winners
2009 Sky Blue FC
2010 FC Gold Pride
2011 Western New York Flash

National Women's Soccer League (NWSL) playoff winners
2013 Portland Thorns FC
2014 FC Kansas City
2015 FC Kansas City
2016 Western New York Flash
2017 Portland Thorns FC
2018 North Carolina Courage

Top league goalscorers (1965–2018)
1965 Herculiano Riguerdo 7
1966 Walter Czychowich 27
1967 Yanko Daucik 20
1968 John Kowalik, Cirilo Fernandez 30
1969 Kaiser Motaug 16
1970 Kirk Apostolidis 16
1971 Carlos Metidieri 19
1972 Randy Horton 9
1973 Warren Archibald, Ilja Mitic 12
1974 Paul Child 15
1975 Steve David 23
1976 Derek Smethurst 20

1977 Steve David 26
1978 Giorgio Chinaglia 34
1979 Giorgio Chinaglia 26
1980 Giorgio Chinaglia 32
1981 Giorgio Chinaglia 29
1982 Ricardo Alonso 21
1983 Roberto Cabanas 25
1984 Steven Zyngul 20
1985 Josue Partillo 8
1986 B. Goulet 9
1987 J. Mihaljevic 7
1988 Jorge Acosta 14
1989 Ricardo Alonso, Mirko Castilo 10
1990 Chance Fry 17
1991 Jean Harbour 17
1992 Jean Harbour 13
1993 Paulinho 15
1994 Paul Wright 12
1995 Peter Hattrup 11
1996 Roy Lassiter 27
1997 Jaime Moreno 16
1998 Stern John 26
1999 Stern John, Roy Lassiter, Jason Kreis 18
2000 Mamadou Diallo 26
2001 Alex Pineda Chacon 19
2002 Carlos Ruiz 24
2003 Carlos Ruiz, Taylor Twellman 15
2004 Eddie Johnson, Brian Ching 12
2005 Taylor Twellman 17
2006 Jeff Cunningham 16
2007 Luciano Emilio 20
2008 Landon Donovan 20
2009 Jeff Cunningham 17
2010 Chris Wondolowski 18
2011 Dwayne De Rosario 16
2012 Chris Wondolowski 27
2013 Camilo Sanvezzo 22
2014 Bradley Wright-Phillips 27
2015 Sebastian Giovinco 22
2016 Bradley Wright-Phillips 24
2017 Nemanja Nikolic 24
2018 Josef Martinez 31

Glossary

Advantage rule A rule that allows the referee to let play continue after a foul if it is to the advantage of the team that has been fouled against.

Anchor A midfielder positioned just in front of and given the job of protecting the defense. An anchor player can help allow other midfielders to push further forward.

Assistant referees Formerly known as linesmen, these officials assist the referee with his decision-making during the game.

Bicycle kick An overhead volley, usually a shot on goal.

Blind side A position on the opposite side of a defender from the ball.

Box The penalty area.

Cap Recognition given to a player for each international appearance made for his country.

Caution Another word for a yellow card.

Chip A ball lofted into the air, either as a pass from a player to a teammate or as a shot. Also known as a lob.

Clearance Kicking or heading the ball out of defense.

Counter attack A quick attack by a defending team after it regains possession of the ball.

Cross Sending the ball from the side of the field toward the opposition's penalty area.

Direct free kick A kick awarded to a team because of a major foul committed by an opponent. A goal may be scored directly from the kick.

Direct play A method of attacking, using long passes from defense that tend to bypass the midfield and go straight to the forwards.

Dribbling Moving the ball under close control with short kicks or taps.

Drop ball A way of restarting the game after a break in play. The referee releases the ball to a player from the team that last touched the ball. All other players must be at least 13 feet away.

Feinting Using fake moves of the head, shoulders, and legs to deceive an opponent and put him off balance.

Formation The way a team lines up on the field in terms of where the defenders, midfielders, and forwards are positioned.

Hand ball The illegal use of the hand or arm by a player.

Indirect free kick A kick awarded to a team because of a minor foul or offense committed by an opponent. A goal cannot be scored directly from the kick, but must instead be played to a teammate first.

Laws of the game The 17 rules of soccer as established and updated by FIFA.

Lay-off A short pass made by a forward to a teammate who is to the side of or behind him.

Libero Another term for a sweeper.

Marking Guarding a player to prevent him from advancing the ball toward the net, making an easy pass, or receiving the ball from a teammate.

Narrowing the angle A goalkeeping technique involving the goalie moving out toward the on-ball attacker to narrow the amount of goal the attacker can aim a shot at.

Obstruction When a defensive player, instead of attempting to win the ball, uses his body to prevent an opponent from playing it.

Overlap To run outside and beyond a teammate down the sides of the field in order to create space and a possible passing opportunity.

Professional foul A foul committed intentionally by a player, stopping an opposition attacker from a clear run on goal.

Set piece A planned play or move that a team uses when a game is restarted with a free kick, penalty kick, corner kick, goal kick, throw-in, or kickoff.

Shielding A technique used by the player with the ball to protect it from a defender closely marking him. The player in possession keeps his body between the ball and the defender.

Square pass A simple pass made by a player to a teammate running alongside him.

Stamina The ability to maintain physical effort over long periods. All players require good levels of stamina to stay effective over an entire game.

Stoppage time Time added to the end of any period to make up for time lost because of a major halt in play, such as treating an injured player. Also known as injury time.

Sweeper A defender that can be played closest to his own goal behind the rest of the defenders or in a more attacking role and who is responsible for bringing the ball forward.

Tactics Methods of play used in an attempt to outwit and beat an opposition team.

Target man A tall striker, usually the player farthest upfield, at whom teammates aim their forward passes.

Through ball A pass to a teammate that puts him beyond the opposition's defense and through on goal.

Video Assistant Referee (VAR) A match offical who reviews decisions made by the head referee by using video footage and a headset for communication.

Volley Any ball kicked by a player when it is off the ground.

Wall A line of defenders standing close together to protect their goal against a free kick.

Wall pass A quick, short pair of passes between two players that sends the ball past a defender. Also known as a one-two.

Weight The strength of a pass.

Zonal marking A system in which defenders mark opponents who enter their particular area of the field.

Websites

The Internet abounds with thousands of websites devoted to particular teams, players, or aspects of soccer, Below, we've detailed some of the most interesting and informative websites currently available.

www.mlssoccer.com
The official website of the MLS league is a fabulous packed collection of history, team data, statistics, news, and opinions. Also included are the rules of the game and coaching advice.

www.clivegifford.co.uk
The author's website, which, under the In-Print section, features regularly updated soccer tips and links to other websites.

www.jbgoalkeeping.com/links.html
For budding goalies, this is the place to head. The website contains many tips and drills for perfecting goalkeeping techniques, as well as a large collection of links to other great goalkeeping websites.

www.fifa.com
FIFA's official site is huge and takes time to surf around. But stick with it because there's tons of data, helpful fact sheets, and the latest version of the laws of the game. There are also links to the governing bodies for soccer in each continent.

www.shekicks.net
Home of the excellent She Kicks magazine, this website is devoted to news and features about women's soccer.

www.nwslsoccer.com
The website of the National Women's Soccer League gives all of the facts, stats, news, and scores from the league, along with full game details.

www.ussoccer.com
The official home on the Internet of U.S. soccer in all its many and various forms. It includes news and results from inside the U.S. leagues and also of U.S. players playing overseas.

www.worldsoccer.com
The online version of World Soccer magazine, this site has news about all the major competitions, plus exclusive player profiles, interviews, and features, as well as the latest games, results, and tables.

www.worldstadiums.com
As its name suggests, this is a site devoted to the venues in which the game of soccer is played all over the world. It is a massive site searchable by country or stadium name.

www.usyouthsoccer.org
The official site of the U.S. Youth Soccer Association, featuring news about young players and their coaches, as well as a list of upcoming competitions and a calendar of events.

www.soccerbyives.net
Solid soccer news website focusing on North American teams, players, and competitions, including international sections.

90soccer.com
The website of one of the leading American soccer magazines contains news, game reports, and other fascinating features.

www.concacaf.com
The U.S. national teams play in the CONCACAF (the Confederation of North, Central American, and Caribbean Association Football) region. This is the organization that runs competitions like World Cup qualifiers and the Gold Cup.

Index

ACKNOWLEDGMENTS

Key: b = bottom, c = center, l = left, r = right, t = top
Photographs in this book have been supplied by Getty, except the following:
Front cover tr, tcr, and cr Ljupco Smokovski/Shutterstock.com; back cover tl, tc, and tr iStock/pat138241; 7bl Shutterstock/sunsinger; 8tl The National Football Museum, cr The National Football Museum, br Corbis, bl The National Football Museum; 9t The National Football Museum, tl Robert Opie Collection, cl The National Football Museum, c The National Football Museum, cr The National Football Museum, bc The National Football Museum, br The National Football Museum; 17c Shutterstock/Beto Chagas, c The National Football Museum, cr The National Football Museum; tr Shutterstock/PrairieEyes; 20tl PA/EMPICS Sport/Tony Marshall; 21c Mitch Gunn/Shutterstock.com; 27br Marco Iacobucci EPP/Shutterstock.com; 33tr Popperfoto; 35tl Shutterstock/ajfi, tc Shutterstock/Christian Bertrand, cr Flickr/Rory Hyde, cl Shutterstock/sunsinger; 57br Shutterstock/maxisports; 70tl Shutterstock/mooinblack, cl Shutterstock/Chanclos, cr Robert Opie Collection, cr Robert Opie Collection; cr www.asroma.it, br pictures courtesy of Sky Sports; 63cl Nationaal Archief Fotocollecti Anefo/Hugo van Gelderen; 71cl Shutterstock/Chanclos; 73cr PA/EMPICS Sport/Matthew Ashton; 74bl Shutterstock/majeczka, br Shutterstock/Paolo Bona; 75tr Allsport UK Ltd/Jamie McDonald, bl Shutterstock/Patryk Kosmider, 80tl, tr www.psg.fr; bc PA/EMPICS Sport/Peter Robinson; 81cl, bl PA/EMPICS Sport/Peter Robinson.